CAMEO CLIFFS
BIKING-HIKING
FOUR-WHEELING

by

F.A. & M.M. Barnes

CAMEO CLIFFS
A recreational paradise on public land
for mountain bikers, day-hikers and
four-wheelers adjacent to
Canyon Rims Recreation Area

CAMEO CLIFFS - "The rest of
Canyon Rims Recreation Area"

"Anywhere else it would have been a national park --
-- and it should have been here, too."

1992
Canyon Country Publications

This book is the TWENTY-EIGHTH in a series
of practical guides to travel and recreation
in the scenic Colorado Plateau region of the
Four Corners States

All written material, maps
and photographs are by the authors
unless otherwise credited

Copyright 1992
Canyon Country Publications
P. O. Box 963
Moab, UT 84532

All rights reserved

ISBN 0-925685-03-8
Library of Congress Catalog Card Number 91-76024

CONTENTS

INSIDE-FRONT COVER .... Map of CAMEO CLIFFS North
CONTENTS 3
FOREWORD 5
INTRODUCTION
    Exploring 7
    Mapping 7
    The Vehicle Trails 8
    Hiking 8
GEOGRAPHY
    The Name 9
    Recreational Use of the Area 9
    Location, Size and Boundary 9
    Elevation 10
    State Land 11
    Private Land 11
HISTORY
    Introduction 13
    Prehistory 13
    Historic Indians 15
    Early Explorations 15
    Settlements 17
    Modern Developments 17
ACCESS
    General Access 23
    Access for Bikers 24
    Access for Hikers 24
    Access for Four-Wheelers 25
    Navigation 25
    The ORV Trails 26
HAZARDS
    General Hazards 27
    Special Biking Hazards 29
    Special Hiking Hazards 29
    Special Four-Wheeling Hazards 30
AESTHETICS 31
SEASONS AND WEATHER
    Seasons 33
    Weather 34
NAMING 36
LOGISTICS
    General 37
    Parking 37
    Supplies 38
    Camping 38
    Useful Maps 39
BIKING 40
HIKING 42
FOUR-WHEELING 46
TRAIL DESCRIPTIONS - CAMEO CLIFFS NORTH 53
TRAIL DESCRIPTIONS - CAMEO CLIFFS SOUTH 89
INDEX OF SIDEBARS 156
INDEX OF ROADS, ORV TRAILS AND HIKING 157
FURTHER READING 158
INSIDE-BACK COVER .... Map of CAMEO CLIFFS South

FOREWORD

CAMEO CLIFFS — Biking - Hiking - Four-Wheeling is a guide for these major forms of popular recreation in a large and beautiful region that lies just east of Canyon Rims Recreation Area. The Bureau of Land Management, the federal agency that administers most of the CAMEO CLIFFS area, originally urged us, as the citizen volunteers who did the field work on Canyon Rims Recreation Area, to include the CAMEO CLIFFS in that recreation area, but our explorations were not done in time.

That belated exploration was, however, completed in 1991. This book is the result. As with Canyon Rims Recreation Area, the CAMEO CLIFFS terrain is park-quality public land but, being "multiple use" land, it has received little protection from natural-resource exploitation. Over the years it has been used and abused by stockmen, uranium prospectors, seismograph operators, pipeline companies and petroleum drillers.

By 1991, however, time and nature had restored some of that damage, although with continuing accelerated soil erosion, leaving most of the area now defined as "CAMEO CLIFFS" almost as wild and unspoiled as it was originally, and making it a wonderful undesignated recreation area.

We hope you enjoy the CAMEO CLIFFS as much as we did while exploring it.

The Authors

Muleshoe Creek.

INTRODUCTION

EXPLORING

For years we, the authors, admired the beauty of the cliffs east of U.S. 191 while traveling toward points south and west, but were always too preoccupied exploring for books about other areas to see what these alluring eastern cliffs had to offer besides their entrancing shape and hue.

In early 1991, while finalizing our definitive book about the BLM's newly expanded Canyon Rims Recreation Area, we began to explore what we had come to call "CAMEO CLIFFS," because the dominant colors of the intricately eroded cliffs reminded us of an old-fashioned pink-and-white cameo locket.

At first, we had hiking in mind, but as we used the few short dead-end ORV trails that we knew about for access to the mysterious, beckoning valleys and giant alcoves formed by the cliffs, then found and drove the long-abandoned seismograph trails that traveled the tops of the lofty peninsulas formed by the convoluted cliff-line, we came to realize that the eroded, rarely-used ORV trails also offered unique opportunities for bikers and other off-road vehicle enthusiasts. We saw that the area would be even more valuable for bikers and four-wheelers who also like to hike, and for hikers who could use the old vehicle trails for access to unique hiking routes and areas.

MAPPING

As we explored the few obvious vehicle trails, we found others, on the ground and on the most detailed U.S. Geological Survey topographic maps of the area, the newest 7-1/2 minute series. Most of the trails were potentially useful to mountain bikers, but a few were not. Some of the trails were good for four-wheeling, but others were either too short or dead end, thus providing little challenge to four-wheelers. Some trails we explored were useless for any kind of recreation. As we explored, we mapped the best trails and omitted those that had no obvious value for biking, four-wheeling or hiking access. The omitted trails are either not shown on the maps in this book, or were not highlighted if they appeared on the USGS maps that served as bases for our maps.

Thus, the trails shown on the maps in this book are not the only ones on the ground. Bikers and four-wheelers who enjoy investigating old mineral-search trails as a form of recreation will find plenty of additional trails to explore, especially in the highlands above and to the south and east of the designated southern area of CAMEO CLIFFS.

THE VEHICLE TRAILS

While most of the vehicle trails that enter CAMEO CLIFFS are short and easy, and many are dead end, the recreation area still has enough such trails to offer something of interest to all kinds of wheeled explorers, including mountain bikers and users of other kinds of off-road vehicles. Most of the vehicle trails are fairly easy, but some will present a challenge to even the most competent bikers and four-wheelers.

The complicated geography and unique beauty of the CAMEO CLIFFS area is barely visible from U.S. 191, the major highway that defines the area's western boundary. The vehicle trails that penetrate it offer closer views, but hiking is necessary for an intimate look at the complex area's unique natural beauty and human history.

Bikers and four-wheelers who prefer to stick to wheels and trails will still find some very interesting, challenging and highly scenic trails to explore. The CAMEO CLIFFS area defined and described in this book has approximately 80 miles of vehicle roads and trails.

There are many other roads and trails to the southeast of CAMEO CLIFFS South, as defined, but that area is heavily used and abused by oil and gas extraction operations and is best avoided. Much of that area is hazardous from leaking poisonous gases and from recent or current road construction and drilling operations. Some of the roads there are posted as unsafe for public use, even though they are on public land.

HIKING

CAMEO CLIFFS is especially delightful for bikers and four-wheelers who like to hike beyond vehicle trails, and for hikers who enjoy exploring wild and beautiful canyon country terrain that few others ever see.

Even hikers who have only standard highway vehicles for access will find outstanding opportunities for free-style hiking within the CAMEO CLIFFS area. In most cases, hikers who do not have vehicles with off-highway capabilities can gain practical access by hiking on the short off-road vehicle trails that penetrate the CAMEO CLIFFS from the perimeter paved highways and graded county roads that provide access to the recreation area.

Hikers who drive low-geared, high-clearance vehicles such as vans or pickups will be able to drive parts of some of the off-road vehicle trails before they park and hike. Refer to the individual road and trail descriptions for details about vehicle access.

GEOGRAPHY

THE NAME

CAMEO CLIFFS was named by the authors. The name was chosen because the pastel colors of the weathered sandstone cliffs that dominate the area bring to mind the old-fashioned pink-and-white cameo locket. The name has no official status with federal or state agencies that administer the public land within its described boundaries.

RECREATIONAL USE OF THE AREA

No permits are required for the recreational use of the area, just common-sense precautions and care while in wild canyon country terrain. With the exception of a few tracts of undeveloped private land, the area is public land, open to public multiple-use. This includes the three popular forms of recreation covered in this book.

LOCATION, SIZE AND BOUNDARY

CAMEO CLIFFS, as described in this book, is entirely within southeastern Utah's San Juan County. The described area lies east of U.S. 191, the paved highway that travels between the towns of Moab and Monticello, immediately adjoining the northern reaches of Canyon Rims Recreation Area. CAMEO CLIFFS is divided into two sections by highway Utah 46 and a natural gap in the cliffline in the vicinity of that paved road.

CAMEO CLIFFS North covers approximately 20 square miles. It is bounded by U.S. 191 on the west, by Utah 46 on the south and by two connecting graded roads on the east, Black Ridge Road and Highline Road, although the southernmost part of the enclosed terrain is a uranium-mining sacrifice area that is now worthless for recreation. The boundary roads that define the two parts of CAMEO CLIFFS North are shown on the area maps depicted on the inside covers of this book. The interior access roads and ORV trails are shown on strip maps throughout the book in appropriate locations.

CAMEO CLIFFS South is approximately 25 square miles in size. It is bounded by U.S. 191 on the west, Utah 46 on the north, San Juan County Road 114 on the south and San Juan County Roads 370 and 116 and an off-road vehicle trail on the east, although the northeastern part of the enclosed terrain is privately-owned ranchland that is off-limits for recreation.

CAMEO CLIFFS thus totals about 45 square miles in size, with most of this area being public land that is accessible to a variety of vehicles and open for public recreation. The entire CAMEO CLIFFS area is within easy range of U.S. 191, Utah 46, SJ 114 or SJ 370. It lies east of a 17-mile stretch of U.S. 191. The recreationally useful part extends not over 4 miles east of U.S. 191 at any point, although two of the roads that define the area are slightly farther east.

ELEVATION

CAMEO CLIFFS ranges in elevation from 5,000 to 6,700 feet, with most of the useful area in the higher part of this range. The lowest part is in CAMEO CLIFFS North, where U.S. 191 crosses Cane Creek Canyon, near the Kane Springs Roadside Rest. The highest part is in CAMEO CLIFFS South, on the rimland adjacent to a survey point called "Rattlesnake" on U.S.G.S. topographic maps. This conspicuous rocky promontory looms above the uppermost end of Joe Wilson Canyon. The peaks of the two heavily mined hills adjacent to Utah 46 are a few feet higher than Rattlesnake but these hills are not accessible for recreational purposes. See a later chapter on how elevation affects the area's climate, seasons and usage for recreation.

Rattlesnake Butte, above Wilson Mesa.

STATE LAND

Several sections of Utah State public land lie within CAMEO CLIFFS. Unless otherwise posted, or leased to private citizens for specific uses and also posted, Utah State land is open to the public for recreational use.

PRIVATE LAND

There are several oddly-shaped tracts of developed and undeveloped private land within CAMEO CLIFFS as defined. In CAMEO CLIFFS North, the Hole-'n-the-Rock tourist development is on private land, as are other developments in Browns Hole, beyond the described stretch of Browns Hole Road. The crude road into the Browns Hole private land is posted and not open to public use.

In CAMEO CLIFFS South, the developed ranchlands in the northeastern corner of the defined area are posted private land, although the numbered and paved county road that goes south through this area is open to public travel. There are also four irregular blocks of private land adjacent to U.S. 191. These are undeveloped beyond a few scattered grazing-support structures that are either abandoned or rarely used.

Since a few of the ORV trails described in this book cross these blocks of private land, the trails could conceivably be closed to travel for recreation, although in most cases these trails are the only practical vehicle access routes into the public land beyond the private land. Thus, the Bureau of Land Management should make arrangements to keep the trails open. If the described vehicle trails are posted or closed, the BLM should be notified.

Any of the ORV trails described in this book that cross undeveloped private land will have notes to this effect in their descriptions.

HISTORY

INTRODUCTION

The history, both early and modern, of the CAMEO CLIFFS area is, for the most part, inextricably entwined with that of the terrain adjacent to it. A more detailed version of that history is presented in the book *Canyon Country's* **CANYON RIMS RECREATION AREA** and other regional history books, including **CANYONLANDS NATIONAL PARK - Early History and First Descriptions.** Following is a brief summary of regional history as it applies to the CAMEO CLIFFS area.

PREHISTORY

There is archaeological evidence of prehistoric Indians of the Anasazi culture hunting and foraging in the CAMEO CLIFFS area, but signs of only very limited early occupation. The many slickrock potholes and spring-seeps, and the seasonal streams in the area, would certainly have supported the large game indigenous to the region at that time, such as deer, desert sheep, elk, probably puma, bear, and antelope, and perhaps bison. These would have been followed by the early hunters who sought them.

In 1987 a prehistoric dwelling was discovered at the base of Cameo Butte. Excavation and study by the BLM revealed a circular pithouse with nine subfloor pits. Tools, projectile points, bones and grinding stones were found at the site, but no pottery shards. Charcoal samples from the site submitted for radiocarbon dating indicated that occupation occurred as early as A.D. 200, explaining the lack of ceramics.

Since the excavation, the only remaining evidence of this ruin is soil stained by ashes. The pithouse was located atop a narrow ridge extending outward from a high and imposing, steep-walled sandstone mesa. The wetter climate of that period must have produced an active spring at the nearby cliff base, providing the pithouse occupants with a viable water source.

More recently, two rockshelter caves were found and reported by the authors in one of the many tributaries of Hook and Ladder Gulch. Although the caves had already been ransacked by vandals, what remained gave testimony to extensive prehistoric use, very likely as burial sites. Large, horizontal colluvium cysts, or concavities in hardpacked ground, and their rock slab "lids," were still visible, and bones and several grinding stones were found. The alcoves are located just above a drainage line that was probably a seasonal stream during the period of occupation.

The entire CAMEO CLIFFS area abounds in beautiful and colorful agate. Prehistoric man must have found this hard and brittle rock very useful for the creation of hunting points and tools. The authors themselves were fortunate in finding a lovely white agate spearhead in the vicinity of the hiking route to Spindle Arch.

Despite the prevalence of smooth sandstone surfaces upon which early man could have left his mark, there are no known petroglyphs or pictographs in CAMEO CLIFFS.

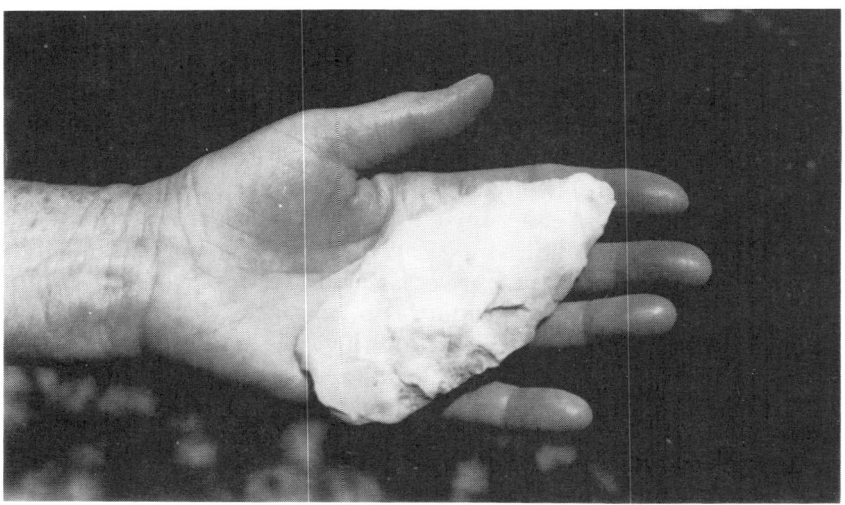

HISTORIC INDIANS

Historic Indians, mostly Utes and Paiutes, hunted in the La Sals and were making encampments in the CAMEO CLIFFS area when the first white settlers arrived.

EARLY EXPLORATIONS

The first record of white men penetrating what is now the state of Utah is in 1765, when Spanish merchant Juan Maria Antonio Rivera sought a route from Santa Fe to California. Two historians contend that his party circumnavigated the La Sal Mountains over its southern flanks, then continued down Moab-Spanish Valley to the Colorado River. These routes would have Rivera passing through the CAMEO CLIFFS area.

These two historians, however, were apparently not aware of the very deeply cut canyons that drain from the La Sals toward the south and southwest. These canyons make it unlikely that men on horseback, with pack mules and a herd of horses, could have taken that route. Further, Rivera's description of his approach to the river does not match the terrain in lower Moab-Spanish Valley. Research by the authors of this book indicates that Rivera probably reached the Colorado River via Castle Valley, and thus did not pass through the CAMEO CLIFFS area. This route does match his description.

The Old Spanish Trail entered Utah at the head of East Wash Canyon just south of CAMEO CLIFFS. For twenty years, from about 1829 to 1845, caravans of Spaniards, Mexicans and others traveled the Spanish Trail, using it as a trading route between New Mexico and California. A deep pothole called *La Tinaja*, used as a water source by the travelers, lies at the base of the landmark monolith, *Casa Colorado*, just south of San Juan 114, which partly defines the southern boundary of CAMEO CLIFFS. Except for an optional side-trip to the *Ojo Verde* watering hole farther west, if *La Tinaja* did not provide enough water for the larger numbers of livestock with some parties, the Trail then advanced northward along the approximate alignment of the present highway, U.S. 191, the western boundary of CAMEO CLIFFS.

In 1859, the Macomb Expedition followed the Old Spanish Trail from Santa Fe, New Mexico, as far as the water hole, *Ojo Verde*. This military mapping and exploring party may have cut across the southern tip of the CAMEO CLIFFS area. For more details about this expedition, refer to the book, **CANYONLANDS NATIONAL PARK - Early History and First Descriptions.**

Besides these, other explorers, including trappers, hunters, miners and stockmen, found their way through the CAMEO CLIFFS area during the late 1800s and the early 1900s, pursuing their respective occupations, but only the bulldozer trails of modern mining and pipelines, and the depleted native grasslands and erosion left by overgrazing, left any permanent scars. White man's names, initials and inscriptions are found in natural caves and on some cliffs near well-traveled routes but, by and large, CAMEO CLIFFS still remains relatively remote, unspoiled and lovely.

Some of the hundreds of historic inscriptions on a cliff at Hole-'n-the-Rock.

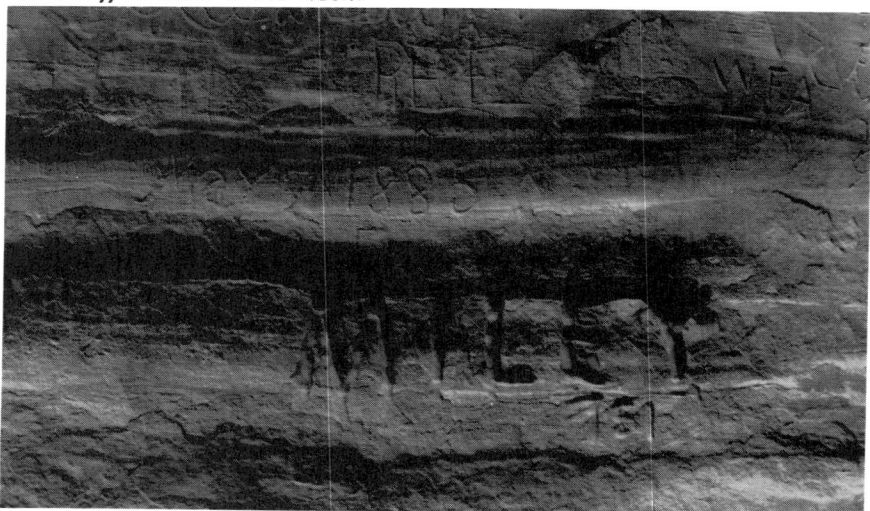

SETTLEMENTS

COYOTE/LA SAL

The only settlement of note near the CAMEO CLIFFS area is the small ranching, farming and mining community of La Sal, named for its geologic neighbor, the laccolithic mountain range to the northwest, named *Sierra de La Sal* (Salt Mountain) by the Spanish. For details on the colorful history of this small town, see the sidebar HISTORY OF LA SAL, UTAH.

BROWNS HOLE

In 1882 an old prospector, "Doby" Brown, settled at a spring about three miles northeast of La Sal Junction. After a few months, he moved to Castle Valley northeast of Moab. The place he abandoned has since been called "Brown's Hole," or "Browns Hole," according to the spelling convention used on modern maps. Since then, Browns Hole has been owned and occupied by a number of people. Although it lies within the CAMEO CLIFFS area, Browns Hole is private land and should not be entered for recreational purposes.

LA SAL JUNCTION

La Sal Junction, where Utah 46 meets Utah 191, formerly served as a popular wayside dining and service stop for ranchers, miners and truckers. The businesses have long since been closed and the buildings deserted, but may be reactivated in the future.

MODERN DEVELOPMENTS

HOLE-'N-THE-ROCK

The only active establishment presently catering to travelers in CAMEO CLIFFS is the Hole-'n-the-Rock tourist development on U.S. 191. For the history of its fascinating construction, see the sidebar ALBERT CHRISTENSEN, SANDSTONE SCULPTOR.

ALBERT CHRISTENSEN
SANDSTONE SCULPTOR

Beginning in 1945, sculptor A. L. Christensen undertook the herculean task of excavating into the side of a great sandstone bluff adjacent to the present highway, U.S. 191. A total of fifty thousand cubic feet of rock was moved to create a cavern home and business establishment, with 5,000 square feet of floor space comprising 14 rooms. He named it "Hole-'n-the-Rock," a more appropriate appellation than for its namesake, the precipitous 1200-foot crevice in solid sandstone down which the 1880 Mormon pioneers lowered their wagons to the Colorado River. After Christensen's death in 1957, his widow Gladys and other family members continued to exhibit the Hole-'n-the-Rock "mansion" as a visitor attraction and memorial. Both A. L. and Gladys are now buried nearby.

Initially, the outer room of the excavation was managed as a restaurant, but in 1955 this business venture was abandoned in favor of a gift shop, which is still in operation. Ten-minute guided tours are conducted of the inner, private rooms of the catacomb-like former abode.

Christensen also put his blasting skills to work carving out big facial images of Franklin Delano Roosevelt and Winston Churchill, with a great, spreadwinged eagle above their heads. This sculpture appeared in a large, open alcove some half a mile south of Hole-'n-the-Rock, fairly close to the gravel road which ran from Moab to Monticello at that time.

Unfortunately for the patriotic artist, the Bureau of Land Management, which administers that particular piece of land, took a dim view of the sculpture and ordered Christensen to erase the great men's visages. He regretfully complied by hacking the features off of the rock face, using a miner's pick. All that remains at the site is the carved frame and barely discernible outlines of the two faces and the eagle, with some unnatural rubble below them -- a pathetic triumph of bureaucracy over art. Pieces of pipe from the sturdy scaffolding the artist built still protrude from the steep sandstone slope below the sculpting, plus several others that indicate there was once a walkway or stairway up to the memorial.

Hole-'n-the-Rock is the best known excavation of its kind in the area, but there are many "cowboy caves" in both CAMEO CLIFFS and nearby Canyon Rims Recreation Area, where dynamite has been employed to create either living quarters or storage facilities for stock feed that would be dry and impervious to rodents. One other formal residence is still under construction in nearby Hatch Rock, on a section of Utah state land. See the sidebar "HATCH ROCK" in the book, *Canyon Country's* CANYON RIMS RECREATION AREA.

CANE SPRINGS

Cane Springs is just north of Hole-'n-the-Rock, and is a shady oasis in a redrock alcove which has been a welcome stop for white travelers in this arid country for more than one hundred and fifty years, and for millennia for Indians. For the first half of this century, the springs served as an important watering hole for cattle on their long drive from ranches in San Juan County to the Thompson's Springs railhead, thirty-seven miles northeast of Moab. It also refreshed those following the Old Spanish Trail, as well as early wagon and stagecoach drivers and passengers, and continues to gratify modern-day tourists as a highway stop misnamed "Kane Springs Roadside Rest." The original name was "Cane Springs." Numerous historic inscriptions attesting to much of this travel appear on the base of the west-facing abutment of the sandstone dome in which Hole-'n-the-Rock was built.

MICROWAVE STATION

The northern boundary of CAMEO CLIFFS is defined by the Black Ridge Road that leaves U.S. 191 and climbs a winding but scenic seven miles to top out at an AT&T microwave relay station. This is one of a series of twelve such stations built in the early 1960s to carry television networks, government circuits and long distance telephone traffic. The system was capable of carrying 1800 phone calls simultaneously across the United States, and the Black Ridge station, as the hub for others in the surrounding area, required a staff of a dozen to operate it.

In recent times, however, usage of this ground-based system has dwindled, thanks to satellite relays and fiber optics, so that only about seven percent of the calls are still handled by the aging system. No longer are personnel assigned to hub maintenance. Thus, it is likely that the system, including the station on Black Ridge, will be phased out in the near future.

But as long as the county road to the tower remains open, CAMEO CLIFFS visitors can still enjoy the magnificent panoramic vistas its terminus affords.

PREHISTORIC AND HISTORIC REMNANTS

Past users of the CAMEO CLIFFS area for various purposes have left evidence of their activities, some obvious, some not. Following is a summary of the kinds of remnants still found.

PREHISTORIC INDIANS. One pithouse, used either as a permanent or seasonal dwelling, and two rockshelter sites, used either for burial or storage, have been found in CAMEO CLIFFS, as well as at least one large lithic point. Doubtless, many other paleolithic points have been found by collectors over the past century, but not reported to the appropriate federal land administration agency. There are no known sites in the area of prehistoric petroglyphs or pictographs.

HISTORIC INDIANS. Historic Indians left little if any evidence of their hunting-gathering use of the CAMEO CLIFFS area.

EARLY EXPLORERS. Spanish explorers left no remnants of their passage through CAMEO CLIFFS except the names they gave to nearby geographic features, such as the La Sal and Abajo mountains, Casa Colorado and the two Spanish Trail waterholes, La Tinaja and Ojo Verde. Other regional Spanish names used by early American explorers did not survive into the present. The 1859 Macomb Expedition left no remnant of its passage within CAMEO CLIFFS proper, but did leave evidence of where the expedition's physician and general scientist, Dr. John S. Newberry, ascended a cliff in nearby East Wash Canyon to an important paleontological find that he made there. Later explorers left no known remnants.

STOCKMEN. The development of agriculture and stock-raising in the general La Sal area, and the heavy grazing of Dry Valley within and to the west of CAMEO CLIFFS, left many remnants of those destructive activities, such as stock ponds, salt licks, abandoned wells, windmills, gasoline-powered pumps, water troughs and tanks, corrals, cattle bones, remnants of early "rip-gut" fences, caves blasted from solid sandstone, miles of barbed wire fences and countless tons of non-biodegradable cattle droppings, plus homesteaded private land. The denudation of the region of native grasses by more than a century of overgrazing, and the resulting drastically accelerated erosion of native soils and changing biological community, was the most damaging and tragic remnant left by stockmen.

PROSPECTORS, MINERS AND DRILLERS. Uranium prospectors and miners left a legacy of bulldozed vehicle trails, only a few of which have any recreational value, plus countless mine shafts, tailings heaps, dugout structures and junk, primarily in the two badly-scarred highlands adjacent to Utah 46 just east of U.S. 191, and in the rugged slopes below Black Ridge. Most of the eroding vehicle trails in these three areas are now worthless for any purpose. The high peninsulas defined by the colorful bluffs of CAMEO CLIFFS are scored by the bulldozed trails of seismographers in the service of the petroleum industry, leaving a legacy of dead trees and eroding trails to nowhere. CAMEO CLIFFS South is crossed by several buried gas pipelines, with still others in the planning stages. The region immediately to the south and east of the CAMEO CLIFFS area as defined has been devastated by past uranium and copper mining and by modern petroleum exploration and development operations.

THE CIVILIAN CONSERVATION CORPS. This pre-World War II government organization, known as the "CCC," had several field camps in southeastern Utah, one just west of U.S. 191 in the CAMEO CLIFFS vicinity. Young men from that camp worked in the area, primarily in support of grazing operations. There are still remnants in CAMEO CLIFFS of small erosion-control dams built by the CCCs, as well as a large concrete-and-rock water tank and windmill near the Old Road Trail in CAMEO CLIFFS North.

EARLY SETTLERS AND SETTLEMENTS. Early settlers left within CAMEO CLIFFS a legacy of private ranchland, some developed and some not, plus the two small developed settlements in the area, La Sal Junction and Browns Hole. Both are still occupied by a few people. The nearby settlement of La Sal is a ranching center with a post office but very little commercial development.

HISTORIC INSCRIPTIONS. Early stockmen and settlers passing through the CAMEO CLIFFS area left a large number of inscriptions on the sandstone mass that now contains the Hole-'n-the-Rock development, on the surface nearest the present highway. Visitors should take care not to damage these historic inscriptions. There are other historic inscriptions in a natural cave at the end of one spur of the Cave Trail, and some badly weathered inscriptions on one of The Nipples, the peaks that top the sandstone dome just north of the junction of U.S. 191 and Browns Hole Road.

EARLY VEHICLE ROADS. There are remnants of two earlier generations of roads in the western fringes of CAMEO CLIFFS North. Where U.S. 191 first descends from the north into the Cane Creek drainage, eroded segments of the original wagon trail are still visible to the east of the highway, while parts of the later graveled automotive road curve around the cliffs to the west of the same segment of highway. South of Hole-'n-the-Rock, several lengths of this second road still follow the meandering cliffline more closely than the modern highway. Within CAMEO CLIFFS North, Cave Trail, Muleshoe Canyon Trail and Old Road Trail travel for parts of their lengths on the old graveled road. The descriptions of these trails provide more details. Several smaller segments of the old road are still visible in both parts of CAMEO CLIFFS.

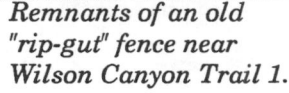

Remnants of an old "rip-gut" fence near Wilson Canyon Trail 1.

U.S. Coast & Geodetic Survey benchmark dated 1933, on the old bridge crossed by Cave Trail.

HISTORY OF LA SAL, UTAH

In 1877, Mr. & Mrs. Tom Ray and their family of eight children, looking for good range and a ranch site, arrived at Coyote Creek at the south side of the La Sals near the site of the present community of La Sal. Although they noted it favorably, with its lovely large spring, they explored some eight miles farther east and found a spot still more to their liking. There they settled on what they named Deer Creek, about a mile southwest of La Sal (now called Old La Sal) which was settled a year later, when relatives and friends of the Rays arrived with their cattle herds and established themselves on Coyote Creek, which was evidently named for the presence of many of these animals in that area.

During their first two years on Deer Creek, the Rays hauled provisions once a year from Salina, Colorado, 200 miles away. Later, they obtained supplies from Durango, 135 miles from (Old) La Sal, where they exchanged locally-produced butter, vegetables and grain with that thriving mining community.

Soon, homesteaders in Moab Valley were bringing in their herds to the extensive ranges on the northeast side of the La Sals to summer there. Others followed from Colorado and other Utah communities and built cabins near the Ray ranch, close enough together to offer some protection from the Indians.

Among those to establish themselves as neighbors of the Rays were the John Silvey family, whose son Frank left a journal of early life in San Juan County, and the La Sal area in particular. THE HISTORY AND SETTLEMENT OF NORTHERN SAN JUAN COUNTY From the Writings of Frank Silvey is available through the Moab TIMES-INDEPENDENT.

In 1878, La Sal was made an outpost on the mail route from Salina, Utah via Moab to Ouray, Colorado, one of the first to be established in southeastern Utah and the adjoining section of western Colorado, and for years was the only mailway -- and a dangerous one. The mail drivers had to make their way through La Sal Divide when winter was at its worst and, during all months of the year, had to keep a constant lookout for hostile Indians.

In 1901 the post office was officially moved from (Old) La Sal to the new headquarters ranch at that time called Coyote. The post office retained the name La Sal and the new ranch and townsite gradually took that name also.

Interface with the local Piutes began immediately upon settlement and for the most part remained peaceful, mainly through the forbearance of the whites -- who were outnumbered ten to one and under-armed. Visits by the natives, both individually and in small groups, were mostly for begging, or for bartering deer hides for food, but with sources of supply being so far away, the whites found it necessary to treat the Piutes with firmness, yet understanding.

In 1880, aberrant behavior on the part of a few Piutes destroyed the tranquility of the village, resulting in the hasty departure of several of its inhabitants. Two young residents, brothers Joe and Ervin Wilson, were attacked by Indians while hunting for stray horses on Black Ridge. The younger boy, Joe, was badly wounded but escaped when friendly Indians helped him back to Moab. He remained crippled and partially blinded for life. For more details refer to the sidebar, "JOE WILSON" in the book, Canyon Country's CANYON RIMS RECREATION AREA. Both Wilson Arch and Joe Wilson Canyon were named in memory of Joe Wilson.

In 1884 a group of Pennsylvania investors, intrigued with tales of the fabulous fortunes to be made in the cattle business, organized the Pittsburg Cattle Company. A representative visited La Sal, bargained with the settlers, and finally bought out the cattle and ranch interests of most of them, including the Rays'. With their investments proving less profitable than they had hoped, the investors hired two young men -- J. M. Cunningham as general manager and Thomas B. Carpenter as ranch foreman -- hoping to improve the operation.

The two were successful and eventually bought out the Pittsburg company. In 1914 they sold the entire ranch, range and stock interests to the La Sal Land and Livestock Company, which hired young Charles Redd as manager. Later Redd was to admit that the first twenty to twenty-five years were difficult ones, but they launched a career measured by its success, expansion and innovation.

Under his management, what was to later become Redd Ranches turned into a vast livestock operation that ranged thousands of sheep and cattle over a huge expanse of public and private land in Utah and Colorado. In later years, when these holdings were divided among Redd's children, the La Sal ranch regained the name of La Sal Livestock under the ownership of Charles Hardison Redd, who still controls the local interests.

For more details about the fascinating life of Charles Redd, refer to the sidebar, "CHARLES REDD, RENAISSANCE MAN," in the book, Canyon Country's CANYON RIMS RECREATION AREA.

Starting in the late 1800s, the La Sals were a magnet for prospectors seeking gold, copper, silver, uranium and platinum. The Big Indian copper discoveries at the south end of the La Sals in 1896 led to a number of other mining ventures. But it was the great uranium rush of the early 1950s that transformed the sleepy ranching village of La Sal into one large trailer haven, with dozens of such temporary homes clustered around each working mine. Whole families resided there, purchasing supplies at the local store and sending their children to the local school. The uranium frenzy lasted through the rest of the 1950s and the entire 1960s, but numerous factors dictated its demise and, once more, La Sal settled back into its former somnolent state.

In 1930, the present townsite of La Sal was firmly established when the former La Sal (now Old La Sal) was abandoned because of frequent floods. The present La Sal boasts a general store with gas pump, a small bakery specializing in pizza, and a post office serving a population of 300. Old La Sal, near Utah 46 farther east, hosts a timber products company and a slowly growing community of private residences.

ACCESS

GENERAL ACCESS

As noted in the chapter on CAMEO CLIFFS geography, the area is defined by certain perimeter federal, state and county roads. Vehicle access into both CAMEO CLIFFS North and CAMEO CLIFFS South is via these same roads, plus branching graded dirt roads that are generally well-maintained by San Juan County.

In CAMEO CLIFFS North, vehicle access is from the paved perimeter roads U.S. 191 and Utah 46, and the graded Black Ridge and Highline roads. A number of off-road vehicle trails spur from these perimeter roads. The graded Browns Hole Road penetrates the area, providing access to still more off-road vehicle trails.

In CAMEO CLIFFS South, vehicle access is via the paved perimeter roads U.S. 191, Utah 46, San Juan 114 and San Juan 370. A number of off-road vehicle trails spur from these perimeter roads. Graded San Juan County roads 116, 181 and 182, plus several other short unnumbered graded roads, penetrate the area, providing access to still more off-road vehicle trails.

The perimeter and interior paved and graded access roads noted above are shown on the maps on the inside covers of this book. The map for CAMEO CLIFFS North is on the inside-front cover. The map for CAMEO CLIFFS South is on the inside-back cover.

The noted paved perimeter roads have all-weather surfaces. The graded perimeter roads are generally kept in good condition, but are subject to occasional rain runoff damage. Caution is suggested while driving graded access roads with standard highway vehicles.

Extreme caution is urged when turning off of U.S. 191 onto any of the described branching graded roads and ORV trails, because there are no turn-lanes and through traffic travels at high speeds. The heavy trucks that now use this highway are especially hazardous to vehicles turning onto obscure ORV trails.

ACCESS FOR BIKERS

Mountain bikers who wish to explore CAMEO CLIFFS off-road vehicle trails, and who drive standard highway vehicles, can park adjacent to the noted access roads where the desired trail begins, then bike that and other connecting trails. When parking beside U.S. 191, it is best to park beyond the fence that borders the highway, closing the gate through the fence. Unless otherwise posted, such highway fences are for cattle-control. They are not intended to bar access to the public land beyond the fences.

Bikers who drive either off-road vehicles, or highway vehicles with higher clearances and low gearing, may wish to drive parts of the perimeter or interior access roads before parking, in order to reach the beginning of a specific ORV trail.

Unloading near The Nipples for the ride on Browns Hole Road and its spur trails.

ACCESS FOR HIKERS

Hikers who drive standard highway vehicles can safely travel the paved perimeter roads at all times, but should exercise caution when traveling perimeter and interior graded roads. In general, all the graded roads noted earlier can be used for hiking access to the beginnings of the described off-road vehicle trails and adjoining hiking areas, but water damage can sometimes require longer walks to reach a specific ORV trail or hiking area.

Hikers who drive various kinds of off-road vehicles can travel any of the CAMEO CLIFFS roads and ORV trails to gain access to desired hiking areas and routes.

ACCESS FOR FOUR-WHEELERS

Those who drive off-road vehicles should have no trouble gaining access to all of the described roads and ORV trails, although some of the described trails are more difficult to travel for some kinds of off-road vehicles. Rain runoff damage has long since made certain ORV trails nearly impassable along certain stretches, providing challenges to driving skills.

NAVIGATION

With the exception of the junction of U.S. 191 and Utah 46, and a few small county road-number signs, none of the perimeter and access roads and ORV trails were designated by signs when this book was being written. Thus, navigation of these roads and trails must be by use of the mileages and other navigational clues provided in the individual trail descriptions in this book. Section maps with these descriptions provide further navigational help, and show the relationships between access roads and various ORV trails.

It is possible that in the future, as use of the CAMEO CLIFFS area for recreation increases, the Bureau of Land Management may decide to place road and trail signs at various junctions, as it has in other nearby canyon country areas.

Most of the perimeter and interior access roads described in this book, and some of the ORV trails, appear on the latest editions of the U.S. Geological Survey 7-1/2-minute series maps, but not all. The names of the five quadrants that cover the CAMEO CLIFFS area are Kane Springs, La Sal Junction, La Sal West, Hatch Rock and Sandstone Draw.

Unfortunately, some of the roads and ORV trails that appear on these U.S.G.S. maps either do not exist on the ground, or are not useful for recreation. Conversely, there are ORV trails on the ground that do not appear on these maps. At this time, the maps in this book are the only ones that show all of the described roads and ORV trails. On these maps, only those ORV trails useful for recreation and described in this book are highlighted.

During the warmer months, a few stretches of the described trails become obscured by seasonal vegetation, making them less visible. Careful use of the maps in this book should serve to overcome this problem, which is especially difficult in late summer and early fall, where trails cross broad, open terrain.

Navigation is especially difficult along a couple of CAMEO CLIFFS trails because they are rarely used, and both wind and rain, in addition to seasonal vegetation, tend to obliterate the trails regularly.

Perhaps heavier use of these trails in the future will make them easier to navigate. On these same trails, stretches of bare slickrock also exhibit few obvious signs of the route. In such places, walking ahead to search out the route is one way to avoid losing the trail on open slickrock.

CAMEO CLIFFS ORV trail users should bear in mind that if a trail is described in this book and appears on an accompanying sectional map, it is on the ground, and the authors have traveled it several times during their explorations for this book. The only exception to this is where heavy flooding might have completely erased sections of trail in major wash bottoms such as Hook and Ladder Gulch. In such cases, following the approximate trail alignment shown on the sectional map should lead to the next stretch of undamaged trail.

THE ORV TRAILS

The ORV trails described in this book are a series of eroded, dead-end, long-abandoned mineral-search routes that are rarely used for anything now. The beautiful terrain through which the trails were originally bulldozed still remains relatively unspoiled, although in a few places the routes of buried petroleum-product pipelines from adjacent areas to the south and east mar the scenery.

Since their original construction decades ago, the ORV trails in the CAMEO CLIFFS area have been used largely for seasonal access by a few hunters and cattlemen. The purpose of this book is to introduce bikers, hikers and four-wheelers to the unique recreational potential of the area.

HAZARDS

GENERAL HAZARDS

As noted earlier, just getting vehicles off of U.S. 191 and onto various branching roads and ORV trails can be extremely hazardous. This will continue indefinitely, since there is little chance that highway turn-lanes will be constructed for recreational users of the CAMEO CLIFFS area.

In the spring and early summer, cattle are grazed on much of the land within CAMEO CLIFFS. These large and awkward animals are hazards in themselves, to both vehicles and people on foot, and their ubiquitous droppings provide additional hazards, as do barbed-wire cattle-control fences and gates across public roads and ORV trails that are difficult to open and close.

During the warmer months, the usual native insects associated with water and certain plant communities present minor hazards, and the exotic flying insects associated with cattle droppings can be extremely annoying.

All native water in the CAMEO CLIFFS area is contaminated by runoff from these droppings, and should not be used without suitable treatment and filtration.

Snakes are occasionally encountered in the more remote areas of CAMEO CLIFFS. Racers and garter snakes are sometimes seen, but rattlesnakes are quite rare, and the native species are small and generally quite reclusive and non-aggressive. Chance encounters can be avoided by being alert.

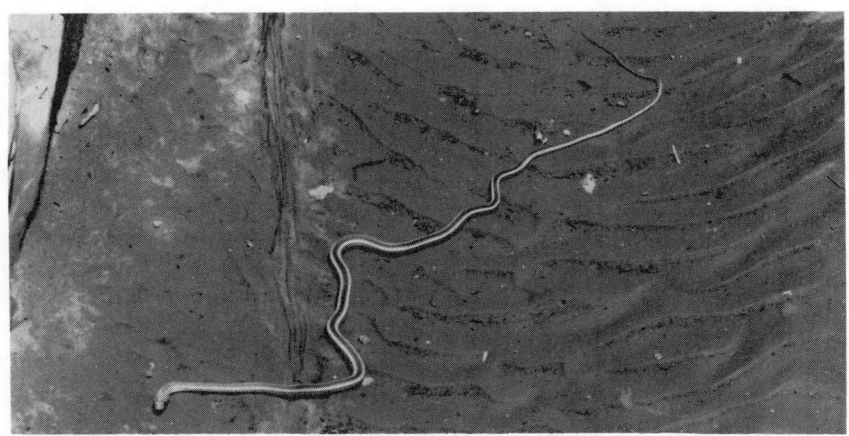

Harmless, fast and beautiful "Desert Striped Whipsnake," Masticophis taeniatus taeniatus, *photographed in upper Hook and Ladder Gulch.*

In some parts of CAMEO CLIFFS inclement weather can be hazardous. Any amount of rain can turn the surfaces of certain graded roads and ORV trails into mud that can be a hazard to driving, and in certain canyons and washes, flash-flooding can result from significant amounts of rain in the drainage areas above them. When storms threaten, heading for higher ground is a reasonable precaution.

High winds can also be hazardous, as in all desert areas. Airborne dust can obscure visibility on vehicle roads and trails, and the powerful updrafts and venturi effects produced by some canyons and rimlands can even affect vehicles and people on foot. The normal warm-season prevailing winds in the CAMEO CLIFFS area, however, are not hazardous, but serve to keep recreationists cool.

During the annual hunting seasons, hunters are extreme hazards. It is advisable for other recreationists to stay out of all canyon country hinterlands during hunting seasons, including the two CAMEO CLIFFS areas. Although this form of recreation is popular, it poses a severe hazard to all other forms of recreation, thus, for practical purposes, converting multiple-use public land into single-use for several weeks each year.

Head for lower ground if a thunderstorm approaches, as here, in upper Joe Wilson Canyon.

SPECIAL BIKING HAZARDS

The general hazards noted above also apply to mountain bikers. The special hazards to mountain biking found in other canyon country areas also occur in CAMEO CLIFFS. Exceptionally steep, eroded ORV trails, sometimes with rough, rocky or sandy surfaces, are the usual hazards. The occasional cattleguards pose another type of hazard.

On some CAMEO CLIFFS ORV trails, nearby sheer drops can be hazardous to bikers who are not cautious, although in most cases the described trails are safe distances from such drops.

The general lack of potable water is especially hazardous to bikers who do not carry an adequate supply. Bikers should not depend on finding potable water anywhere within CAMEO CLIFFS, nor is it wise to count on sources that could be chemically purified, although in some seasons, or following local rain, rainwater can be found in many shallow potholes. There are several dripping springs in the area, but these are accessible only to hikers, and may not produce useful quantities of water year-around. The best plan for bikers is to carry along all the water that might be needed, plus about 50% extra as a precaution.

SPECIAL HIKING HAZARDS

In addition to the general hazards noted earlier, hikers must be especially alert when hiking near the rims of the sheer cliffs that dominate the CAMEO CLIFFS highlands. Most such cliffs have great quantities of loose agate rubble and pebbles lying around, agate that has eroded from the softer sediments that top the sandstone cliffs.

Hikers should also be especially alert for the tiny rattlesnake species that are native, but quite rare, in this region. During the year that the authors of this book were exploring the CAMEO CLIFFS area at least two days a week, they did not see a single rattlesnake.

Hikers who explore the area's many lovely eroded slickrock masses should also be careful not to attempt descending slopes that are too steep, or that cannot be climbed, without assurance that continued progress below the slope is possible. This can be a hazard when exploring certain slickrock canyons in the CAMEO CLIFFS area.

For a detailed introduction to the special skills involved in hiking this region's sandstone slickrock, refer to the book, ***Canyon Country SLICKROCK HIKING & BIKING.***

SPECIAL FOUR-WHEELING HAZARDS

In addition to the general hazards listed earlier, four-wheelers must be especially cautious where ORV trails travel near vertical or steep drops. Several of the described trails pass quite close to such cliffs. Drivers who carefully stay on the described trails should be in no danger.

Some of the described ORV trails are also highly eroded by rain runoff along certain stretches. These especially eroded areas are generally noted in the individual trail descriptions, but drivers should always be alert because each severe rain storm, or even rapid snow-melt in early spring, can produce new trail hazards.

As with other off-road vehicle trails in canyon country, four-wheeling drivers exploring CAMEO CLIFFS trails should remain always alert to trail conditions, because the only maintenance they receive is that done by their occasional users.

View from a slickrock stretch of the Cameo Ridge Trail.

AESTHETICS

The CAMEO CLIFFS recreation area is relatively small compared to other designated special areas in canyon country, but it is outstandingly beautiful in several very special ways. Those traveling along U.S. 191 can catch a glimpse of this beauty, but only a glimpse. To really sample the unique and special aesthetics of the two separate areas of CAMEO CLIFFS, it is necessary to penetrate them with wheels or on foot, then explore further on foot beyond where wheels can go.

The colorful cliffs visible from most of the area's perimeter roads are just part of the aesthetic scene. Within the area, invisible from the perimeter roads, are numerous other spectacular and colorful panoramas, mazes of deep slot canyons, rows of gigantic spring-seep alcoves, lofty masses of beautifully eroded red-hued sandstone, giant dry-waterfall pouroffs, unusual natural arches and bridges, hidden springs and pools and an endless variety of especially lovely hidden natural places.

Observant hikers will encounter countless things, large and small, that will contribute to their aesthetic enjoyment, among them the eroded cameo-colored Entrada Sandstone cliffs, peninsulas and buttes; the water-carved white Navajo Sandstone canyons and grottoes in CAMEO CLIFFS South; the banded Morrison Formation terracing above the cliffs; countless ancient and gnarled pinyons and junipers; the lovely shapes of several natural rock openings, both arches and bridges; and countless spires, giant spring-seep alcoves, fins and buttes shaped by erosion over eons of time from the colorful sandstone cliffs.

Exploring CAMEO CLIFFS allows views of these aesthetic highlights from many angles, and during the varying lighting of different times of the day. Hiking allows closer examination of the colorful terrain, the massive amounts of beautifully colored agate that occurs many places, and myriad less conspicuous aesthetic delights.

In addition to these major aesthetic features within CAMEO CLIFFS are the spectacular vistas of nearby mountain ranges, and the picturesque open meadows, sageflats and geologic prominences in Canyon Rims Recreation Area to the west of the highway. From the tips of the several lofty peninsulas in CAMEO CLIFFS, features to the west can be seen as though from an aerial viewpoint.

The seasons, and even the changing weather that occurs throughout the year, also afford a variety of aesthetic experiences, as the moody lighting of lower angled sunshine, the patterns of cloud shadows, the bands of descending rain or the chromatic beauty of fall colors augment the already spectacular settings of CAMEO CLIFFS.

Altogether, CAMEO CLIFFS is an aesthetic experience supreme. The area is a landscape photographer's dream, a naturalist's paradise, a poet's inspiration.

SEASONS AND WEATHER

SEASONS

The four seasons are much the same in CAMEO CLIFFS as in other parts of Canyon Country, except a little milder during the summer due to the area's somewhat higher elevation range.

The lower parts of CAMEO CLIFFS, where elevations vary between five and six thousand feet, are accessible a month or so earlier in the spring than the higher parts, but are a little warmer during the summer.

In the spring, which sometimes arrives as early as February in the region, exploring CAMEO CLIFFS is delightful, although the changeable weather of March and April often brings surprises. Then, spring wildflowers add to the beauty of the area's broad meadows and drainages, cool breezes make hiking comfortable, and passing clouds grace the clear blue skies.

Once the higher slopes and peninsulas are accessible, when the longer-lasting winter snow has melted and the roads and ORV trails have dried to passable condition, these areas are cooler, affording more comfortable recreation during the period when lower parts of Canyon Country are sometimes uncomfortably warm.

In the fall, the first lasting snow generally does not arrive until November, or in some years December, making autumn the ideal time of the year for exploring CAMEO CLIFFS. The prevailing winds calm, leaving the cooler days ideal for hiking.

Some winters, when the snowfall is light, the canyons and alcoves of CAMEO CLIFFS that are accessible from U.S. 191 can be explored, either on foot or using off-road vehicles. If the scant snow and moist ground are well-frozen, even biking can be pleasurable in the winter, although the daylight hours are short.

WEATHER

CAMEO CLIFFS weather varies with the seasons, as it does in the rest of southeastern Utah's canyon country. The elevation range, from 5,000 to 6,700 feet, also affects the area's weather, although not by much. The winters bring more snow to the higher rimlands, and the summers are warmer on the lower elevations. Otherwise, the weather through CAMEO CLIFFS is about the same throughout its elevation range.

In the early spring, February through April, the dominant weather is cool and windy, with some localized precipitation, either rain or snow, but the snow doesn't last long. Spring weather is changeable, frequently shifting from calm, sunny and delightful, to cool, overcast and windy, sometimes within the same day.

Because of the meandering clifflines that dominate CAMEO CLIFFS, and the strange effects these have on winds, the spring winds can be uncomfortable to hikers and bikers who prefer calmer weather, but normally should have no ill effect on four-wheeling. On the other hand, hikers and bikers do not often have to contend with heat during the spring months.

The late spring months, May and June, are usually more predictable, although this varies from year to year. The winds are generally calmer, there are fewer storms, and the days are sunnier. With its generally higher elevation range, the CAMEO CLIFFS area is usually ideal for hiking and biking in late spring, and also quite suitable for four-wheeling.

The summer months, July and August, are usually quite warm throughout the high-desert canyon country, but in the higher elevations of CAMEO CLIFFS the heat is generally less and more bearable due to the prevalence of gentle breezes. The surface topography of the land to the south and west of the area evidently creates more air movement, making recreation there less subject to summer heat. In sum, when it gets uncomfortably warm in the lower elevations of canyon country for more physically active recreation, CAMEO CLIFFS is one good place to go.

The autumn months, September through November, usually have the mildest weather of the season, although as the days grow shorter and the nights longer, average daytime temperatures gradually drop. At worst, however, with the rare exception being an occasional passing storm front, fall weather is delightful, ideal for hiking, biking, four-wheeling and other types of recreational activities and special interests.

Fall days, with their lower, more dramatic lighting and the added patina of autumn-blooming annual wildflowers and perennial shrubs, have an almost magical aura to them, a mood that is captivating and enchanting, and a chromatic beauty that makes photographers mutter to themselves and run out of film.

The winter months, December and January, usually bring enough snow to CAMEO CLIFFS that recreation there is limited to those who enjoy wintertime hiking, but since many of the ORV trails that penetrate the area are easily accessible from all-weather perimeter roads, and few of them are very long, winter hiking can be delightful.

Then, the patina of snow that usually clings to all fairly horizontal surfaces, except in sunnier exposures along the bases of reflective cliffs, adds still another element of color to an already outstandingly colorful area. Further, daytime warming usually brings some melting of the snow. The seeping water wets the red-hued sandstone, making its colors still richer, and in greater chromatic contrast to the white of the ice-crystal-encrusted snow. Winter is a good time for hiking in CAMEO CLIFFS.

NAMING

As noted earlier, CAMEO CLIFFS was named by the authors because the pastel hues of the dominating Entrada Sandstone cliffs resemble the pink-and-white of an old-fashioned cameo locket.

In order to write about and describe the various ORV trails and natural features in the area, the authors had to name these too, wherever they had not been named on the latest U.S.G.S. topographic maps. The naming task was further complicated by the fact that some named natural features, such as "Hook and Ladder Gulch" or "Muleshoe Canyon," were not simple canyons but complex drainages with several major upper canyons.

For example, Hook and Ladder, as it goes beneath U.S. 191 about 3-1/2 miles south of Wilson Arch, is comprised of more than twenty significant branch drainages, some of them quite large and none of them with names of their own.

In addition, as the authors explored the many trail-less areas of CAMEO CLIFFS, they found a number of sizable natural arches and bridges that had never before been reported. These, too, were given names. The various off-road vehicle trails were also named for practical reasons. While these names are not "official," perhaps in time they will be accepted by other users, and BLM recreation planners will provide trail signs using this nomenclature, as an aid to navigation, as they have in other canyon country areas.

Thus, in the matter of geographic names, this book uses official names where they exist, and its authors have assigned names where they do not, but are needed for practical purposes. As this book was written, these assigned names appear only in this book, but perhaps in time they will be adopted by users and various authorities and thus become "official."

One-Eye Window.

LOGISTICS

GENERAL

CAMEO CLIFFS can be explored from either Moab or Monticello, from public campgrounds in nearby Canyon Rims Recreation Area, or from primitive campsites within CAMEO CLIFFS. CAMEO CLIFFS North is nearer to Moab, while CAMEO CLIFFS South is about midway between the two towns. Both towns offer a variety of commercial overnight accommodations.

Although La Sal and La Sal Junction would be convenient to both areas of CAMEO CLIFFS, neither offers traveler amenities at this time, although limited supplies and automotive fuel are available at La Sal during weekdays.

PARKING

As discussed briefly earlier, hikers and bikers who intend to ride or hike any of the ORV trails in CAMEO CLIFFS can park near the starts of the trails, but not on the highway right-of-way along U.S. 191 or any other numbered state or county road. Along the federal highway, there is usually plenty of room for parking that is safe for standard vehicles just beyond the gates that provide access through the highway cattle-control fences.

Unless otherwise indicated in this book, the land beyond the highway fences is public land that is open to public use.

On paved state roads, or on paved or graded county roads, there are usually plenty of places to drive well off of the right-of-way in the vicinity of the branching graded road or ORV trail that is to be hiked or biked. Four-wheelers, of course, do not have parking problems.

In CAMEO CLIFFS backcountry, those who have high-clearance, low geared vehicles, and who use them to travel part of the way along the poorer graded roads or the better ORV trails, should also park well clear of the road or trail. There are usually many convenient pullouts, although some may have surfaces that are sandy and soft. Drivers of highway-type vehicles should be wary of this.

SUPPLIES

Food, water, fuel and other outdoor supplies are readily available at either Moab or Monticello. Limited supplies are available at La Sal on weekdays and in Canyon Rims Recreation Area at the commercial resort near the entrance to the Needles District of Canyonlands National Park.

Because the major sources of supply are not close enough to be convenient, those wishing to spend several days exploring the trails and backcountry of CAMEO CLIFFS, should take along all the provisions that will be needed.

CAMPING

There are commercial campgrounds at Moab and Monticello and at the entrance to the Needles District of Canyonlands National Park that can serve as bases from which to explore CAMEO CLIFFS.

Two public campgrounds are located in nearby Canyon Rims Recreation Area. Wind Whistle Campground is beside the Needles Overlook Road, about 6 miles west of U.S. 191. Hatch Point Campground is near Anticline Overlook Road, about 8 miles north of the Needles Overlook Road. Both provide convenient access to CAMEO CLIFFS South, but are somewhat farther from CAMEO CLIFFS North, which is best explored from Moab. For a listing of other developed campgrounds in the general vicinity, refer to the book, *Canyon Country* **CAMPING**.

Numerous places within CAMEO CLIFFS are suitable for primitive camping. Since most of the area is public land, backcountry campers need only choose an appropriate, convenient site. There are many such sites beside the various graded roads and ORV trails. Backpackers will find even more lovely sites, far from any vehicle roads or trails, but should take care not to camp in or too near drainages that might flood following a rain.

All who choose to camp within CAMEO CLIFFS should select sites that have already been used, or sites that will minimize damage to native vegetation and cryptogamic soils, the rough-surfaced crusts that protect the sandy soils in this region from wind and rain erosion. Experienced canyon country campers always choose either bare soil or smooth patches of slickrock for camping, always leave their campsites clean, use only dead and down trees for firewood, and are cautious with fire. They do not bury or burn trash. They also follow good backwoods sanitation practices, by burying their body wastes deeply, and far away from drainage lines.

USEFUL MAPS

The only maps needed for exploring CAMEO CLIFFS are those in this book, including the area maps on its inside covers and the detailed strip maps near the various ORV trail descriptions.

Conventional highway maps are useful for reaching the general vicinity of CAMEO CLIFFS, but are of little value for practical access. The U.S.G.S. metric series maps are much the same. Neither kind of map shows all the described access roads and few if any of the ORV trails. The older U.S.G.S. 15-minute series of topographic quadrants is equally obsolete.

The entire CAMEO CLIFFS area is shown on five 7-1/2 minute U.S.G.S. topo maps. These are Kane Springs, La Sal Junction, La Sal West, Hatch Rock and Sandstone Draw in the new series maps. As noted earlier, not all of the roads and trails shown on the maps in this book are on these U.S.G.S. maps, but they are useful to hikers who wish to explore the area in depth.

BIKING

As noted in the foreword, most CAMEO CLIFFS trails are dead-end, but several make connections with other roads or trails and are thus continuous. Others can make large loops, beginning and ending at widely separated points on perimeter or internal roads, thus requiring vehicle shuttles. Several others can be traveled to make loops that return to the same starting point, making such shuttles unnecessary.

Trail surfaces vary from firm, easy and level, to steep, sandy, eroded, rough, ledgy and rocky, even within a single trail, so trail surfaces are not described in detail in trail descriptions, except the few that present special problems. Reduced tire pressure will make sandy and rough trails easier.

Most trails are far easier for mountain bikes than for four wheeled vehicles, yet present a continuing challenge because of the varied terrain and trail surfaces. Several trails present navigational problems because of seasonal vegetation in open stretches. Others are complicated by too many old mineral-search trails made by over-enthusiastic 'dozer operators.

Some trails have adjacent areas of bare slickrock that offer excellent opportunities for free-style slickrock biking and gymnastics.

Late evening slickrock biking near the Dragonview Trail.

40

The mileages given in the trail descriptions were measured by vehicle travel using a trip-meter, but should be considered only approximate since all bike and motor-vehicle odometers vary in accuracy. For optimum trail navigation, bikers should use the topographic strip maps in this book, plus the mileages and landmarks given along each road and ORV trail described.

The trails described are all on public land except where specifically noted otherwise in a very few places. All the fences encountered along the roads and ORV trails are for the control of cattle grazing on public land. Leave the gates through them as found -- open or closed. The public lands are used for grazing only seasonally. The cattle are moved to and from higher elevations as the seasons progress.

Thus, in late winter and early spring, there are cattle in the lower areas of CAMEO CLIFFS, but in the warmer months the cattle are gone and gates can be left open. The exceptions to this are gates through highway fences, which should be kept closed at all times to prevent any remote possibility of animals straying onto the busy highway and causing accidents.

HIKING

Hiking for bikers and four-wheelers can be from and beyond the described roads and trails, as indicated in each description. Hiking for non-bikers and non-four-wheelers is first on the ORV trails, then as described from these trails, although hikers with high-clearance, low-geared highway vehicles may be able to travel some of the ORV trails for short distances before starting their hikes.

Except for the hikers who must hike the ORV trails for access, all hiking is free-style and trail-less, through primitive terrain, although sometimes deer trails and cattle trails offer easier routes through densely wooded areas. In most areas, staying on exposed sandstone wherever possible permits steady progress through otherwise heavily overgrown terrain.

Conscientious hikers will choose routes that minimize damage to the area's profuse cryptogamic crusts that hold the sandy soils together and resist erosion, by hiking on exposed rock and following drainage lines wherever possible, or walking on the litter beneath the larger trees.

Suggested specific hiking routes are noted in individual road and trail descriptions, but in general hikers should follow drainage lines or the bases of clifflines, wherever this is possible, and explore up onto sandstone shoulders, slopes, terraces and fins as high as practical, for interesting distant views, unusual erosional features and isolated plant communities. For variety, hikers can return to their bikes or other vehicles via different routes.

In higher terrain, the best hiking is near cliff-rims for easiest progress, for minimal cryptogam damage, and for the best views below of erosional features. Younger and older hikers who are less sure-footed should beware of dangerous drops along cliff rims and when climbing slickrock slopes. In case of injury or other trouble, help is not readily accessible from the cliff-rims of CAMEO CLIFFS.

While hiking the eroded slickrock slopes and terraces along cliff bases, hikers should try to go everywhere possible without endangering the least capable hikers. A certain amount of careful free-climbing helps attain otherwise inaccessible levels. For this kind of slickrock exploration, good hiking boots are essential, tough leather gloves are useful and a length of stout rope can be helpful with less sure-footed hikers. Since CAMEO CLIFFS is high-desert terrain, hikers should consider sun hats and dark glasses essential any time of the year, plus the use a high-rated sunscreen lotion.

For additional locations good for slickrock hiking, see the guidebook, *Canyon Country* **SLICKROCK HIKING AND BIKING.**

All the hiking routes suggested under the trail descriptions were explored by the authors, but hikers will be able to find many other routes and highlights by creative exploring. One large area that lies between two described trails offers several square miles of prime wilderness hiking.

See the sidebar, CAMEO CLIFFS HIKING, for some of the things to watch for while exploring this outstanding recreation area.

CAMEO CLIFFS HIKING

To most people, the term "hiking" is associated with ideas or memories of clearly defined trails through the woods or up gentle mountain slopes, with direction signs at trail junctions, more signs giving the names of trees or bushes or nearby mountains, designated campsites at intervals and, of course, the final destination, such as a lake or river or mountain meadow or special geologic feature, for which the hike was made.

To hike such typical trails, hikers expect to travel in groups and slog along steadily, pausing only now and then to read the little signs or take a quick picture or take a breather or head for one of the little unisex latrines placed at intervals, until that ultimate destination is reached.

Hiking in CAMEO CLIFFS is not like that. There are no manicured trails, no little signs, no designer pit-stops, no designated campsites and, above all, no special destinations. All of CAMEO CLIFFS is special, and the only ultimate goal is to get safely back to your vehicle before dark falls. There are, however, natural routes which hikers can travel -- until some other direction looks more interesting.

Hiking in CAMEO CLIFFS is not for the destination oriented. Just the opposite. The only way to savor and appreciate what there is to see in this wondrous area is to poke around, wander here and there, explore this or that, stop and study whatever looks interesting, photograph what looks lovely, amble along a sandstone ledge or ridge, climb a slickrock slope, inch along an elevated terrace, trace a deer trail, head up a narrow canyon, climb into every seep-cave, inspect every inch of a cameo-hued wall of smoothly-eroded rock that looms hundreds of feet above the colorful complexity of an inner gorge.

And while you are pursuing this antithesis of conventional hiking, there is no end of things to watch for, things large and small, things obvious and not so obvious, things common here but rare elsewhere, things that are mysterious, colorful, weird, lovely, unique, underfoot, overhead, living, non-living, dead or dying, things of the past or future. And keep asking yourself questions like what? and why? and how? and when? and who? and --

Well, you get the idea. Just wander around in this little part of a big high-desert region and absorb its every detail into your mind, your feelings, your meat and bones.

Make its unique beauties a part of your lifetime memories. You will go away a better person, with a renewed zest for life. CAMEO CLIFFS does that to people who watch for --

-- distant panoramas and nearby scenes and cryptogamic soils and porcupine scat and the strange color-banding of aeolian sandstone --

-- and ancient juniper trees and piles of empty pinyon nut shells on a boulder and badger holes in sandy slopes and shards of colorful agate --

-- fallen from lofty cliffs and lying around on slickrock slopes, in sandy washes and wedged in narrow canyons --

-- dripping springs and passing clouds born of the Abajos and tiny pothole rock gardens and cacti flat and barrel-shaped with buds or glorious blooms or pods of tiny black seeds --

-- and the petrified tracks of ancient creatures long reverted to dust, and the myriad sandstone ledges in myriad arid drainages, each with its own unique shape --

-- and the countless ornately rounded holes in some sandstone walls and the messy nests raptors build on elevated cliff ledges --

-- little "Entrada berries," those marble-sized spheres of sandstone that accumulate in heaps here and there, the "concretions" that geologists can't explain --

-- and potholes large and small, shallow and deep, in rows like concave beads, and hummingbirds who are attracted to red shoelaces --

-- the wads of sticky resin under wounded pinyon trees and the intricate patterns of insect and bird and animal tracks in sandy washes --

-- and the small hawks whose worried cries echo from the canyon walls --

-- and everywhere the mosses, mostly dark and dormant and waiting for a bit of rare moisture, but some bright green where seeping water gives it life --
-- mosses in spring-seeps, mosses on bare rock, mosses on arid soil surfaces, mosses almost everywhere, the most ubiquitous but inconspicuous plant in the area --

-- except perhaps the lichen, gray and lime green and red and yellow and pale blue and orange and dead --
-- the white lichen are the bleached mineral skeletons left behind when the going got too tough even for these ancient and primitive plants --

-- and in the three warmer seasons watch for the wildflowers that favor each, the richer colors early from spring rains, the brighter yellows and whites after late-summer rains --

-- listen for the yap-yap of a territorial male coyote, or the talking-growl of a coyote mother warning of a nearby den of pups --

-- then there are the seep-caves, small, medium, large and gigantic, some with rows of tiny plants in the seeps, many mostly arid, a very few with no ends at all, making natural windows --

-- and where thriving cottonwoods and exotic tamarisk indicate secret underground water, where box elder grow in wetter patches and the rare cluster of cattails in tiny marshes --

-- watch for hardy, still-living trees standing on tip-toe, where the soils have been eroded from beneath them, or rockfalls have left them hanging from a ledge or cliff --
-- and other trees clinging to life by a single root, after being stranded on a ridge of solid rock --

-- the tragedy of ancient desert soils eaten away by the eco-murder of overgrazing, of any grazing at all in the arid pinyon-juniper life zone --
-- or the strange places where tiny pinyons have chosen to take root, or have tried, or the almost symbiotic compatibility of pinyon and juniper trees --

-- and the graceful sweeping patterns left in sand by the blowing grass stems and twigs, and the notches worn in rock by trees that have grown too close to sandstone walls --

-- and arches large and small, lovely and homely, and arches-in-the-making that will get there almost any millennium now --

-- and the Ponderosa pines that are remnants of ages and climates past, as are the lichen and cryptogams, and the pothole life that appears magically now and then in sandstone hollows --

-- and hawks and ravens and eagles and wrens and magpies and whip snakes and lizards and owls and the signs of bats and mud swallows and chipmunks and packrats and - yes - families of little ducklings in Muleshoe Creek in the spring --

-- and yucca plants of several sizes, but all with pointed dispositions, and a rare patch of poison oak --

-- and the sweeping lines of soaring, cameo-hued sandstone cliffs, with towers and crenelations and abutments and fins and promontories and alcoves and overhangs and undercuts and terraces, all sculpted into myriad shapes as only possible by the artistry of time and water and wind and the patient, subtle workings of lichen and mosses and microlife of other sorts.

These, and a billion other equally meaningful things, are what CAMEO CLIFFS is all about.

FOUR-WHEELING

The shorter ORV trails in CAMEO CLIFFS are primarily useful for biking and for hiking access, but some of the longer trails are worth exploring by even the most avid four-wheelers. One moderately difficult and challenging loop route is available in CAMEO CLIFFS South.

Some CAMEO CLIFFS trails are so rough and eroded that it is advisable to lower ORV tire pressure for ease of travel and better traction. Tire pressures of 6 to 15 psi are recommended, depending on the type of vehicle and its gross weight -- the lighter the vehicle, the lower the tire pressure. Tires should be re-inflated to highway pressure, using either a manual or electric pump, before traveling on paved roads.

Most of the ORV trails in CAMEO CLIFFS can be traveled with little difficulty by the average driver, but a few are so broken, eroded and steep that exceptional driving skills are needed. One trail can be traveled its full length only in one direction, because one short stretch is so steep it is essentially one-way for motor vehicles. With ORV trails that have difficult or one-way stretches, this is indicated in the **DIFFICULTY** section of their descriptions.

There are more trails, that are not described in this book, in the heavily mined areas in the southern part of CAMEO CLIFFS North and the northern part of CAMEO CLIFFS South, as well as in the higher terrain to the south and east outside of CAMEO CLIFFS. Most of these trails are not scenic, and many are too highly eroded and rocky for enjoyable four-wheeling.

CAMEO CLIFFS WILDLIFE

Wildlife abounds in CAMEO CLIFFS although, as in all such high-desert areas, much of it is nocturnal and rarely seen. Most of the animal species found in adjacent Canyon Rims Recreation Area also occur in CAMEO CLIFFS.

Mule deer, coyotes, foxes, badgers, porcupines, bobcats and a wide variety of birds, rodents, snakes, lizards and a few amphibians inhabit CAMEO CLIFFS. Hawks, ravens and golden eagles nest on lofty ledges in the miles of cliffs. Bats spend the daylight hours in crevices in the same cliffs. Owls nest and roost in the many remote canyons, and hunt the open spaces at night.

The area also hosts a variety of insects, such as beetles, flies, spiders, wasps, and other less well known species, although many are nocturnal and the only signs of their presence are trails of tiny foot tracks left in sandy washes, or little heaps of soil-pellets piled up around nest-holes in the ground. There are also ants of several sizes and species, and the pyramidal heaps of debris from their underground nests, centered in little circular clearings, are common. The area's few ponds and seeping springs host water-loving insects such as dragon flies, water striders, mosquitoes, and others.

The occasional slickrock potholes that hold water for long enough sometimes host cryptobiotic life, those rare insects and crustaceans whose egg or larval forms can survive years of heat and dehydration in the shallow sediments in pothole bottoms, then revive and continue their life cycles when conditions are right.

During their explorations, the authors of this book personally observed mule deer, coyotes, jack rabbits, cottontails, chipmunks, ground squirrels, pocket squirrels, a variety of lizards, whipsnakes, and garter snakes, redtail and barred hawks, smaller hawk species such as kestrels, golden eagles, large owls, ravens, magpies, many smaller birds and a species of toad, but saw plentiful signs of badgers, skunks, porcupines, foxes, packrats and bobcats. Midget Faded and Hopi rattlesnakes exist in the area but are rare, small and unaggressive. Observant hikers will see countless foot tracks of wildlife in the sandy soils, dune sand and sandy washes of the area.

As in the rest of high-desert canyon country, many CAMEO CLIFFS species that are nocturnal during the warmer months, become diurnal during the cold winter months. Then, the smaller prey species venture out only during the warmer sunlight hours, and the predators that seek them are forced to do the same.

For more details about canyon country wildlife, refer to the books, *Canyon Country* HIKING and *Canyon Country's* CANYON RIMS RECREATION AREA.

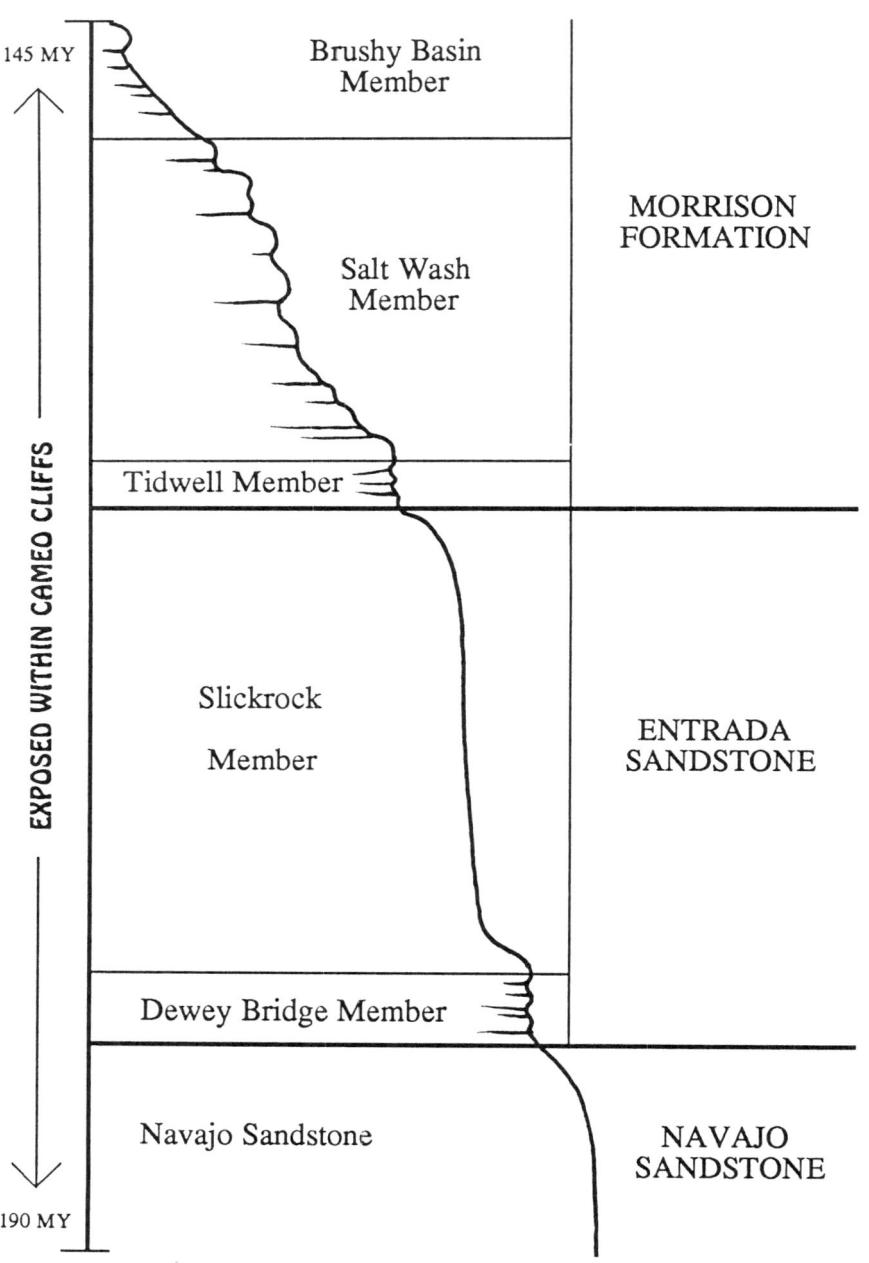

CAMEO CLIFFS GEOLOGY

The geology of the two adjacent areas defined as CAMEO CLIFFS North and CAMEO CLIFFS South is relatively simple, yet cannot be separated completely from the more complex geologic structures that surround them.

The geologic strata in the CAMEO CLIFFS area are few and easily defined and observed. Their basic sequence has been disturbed only to a minor extent by a fault just north of the Kane Springs Roadside Rest.

The geologic strata exposed in CAMEO CLIFFS range from about 190 to 145 millions years in age. These are, from the oldest to the youngest: Navajo Sandstone, Entrada Sandstone and the Morrison Formation, all from the Jurassic Period.

Navajo Sandstone is a massive aeolian sandstone that is basically desert-dune deposits. It is generally white in the CAMEO CLIFFS area. It is not exposed in CAMEO CLIFFS North, but is exposed in CAMEO CLIFFS South in the bottoms of the Joe Wilson Canyon, Hook and Ladder Gulch and Sandstone Draw drainages, where water erosion has cut into it, forming white inner canyons. There are also exposures of Navajo Sandstone in the upper drainages of Hook and Ladder Gulch and Sandstone Draw, and on the narrow ridgeline that separates them.

Entrada Sandstone in the CAMEO CLIFFS area is divided into two distinct parts. These are, in the order deposited: the Dewey Bridge Member, which is a dark red mudstone layer only a few feet thick, and the Slickrock Member, which is largely aeolian, or dune sand, and quite thick. There is a third part of the Entrada, the Moab Member, that is prominent farther north but not found in the CAMEO CLIFFS area. The massive, colorful cliffs after which the recreation area was named are Entrada Slickrock sandstone, standing on a base of the Dewey Bridge Member.

The Morrison Formation is also three-part. In order of deposit, these are: the Tidwell Member, a reddish mudstone that is only a few feet thick in the CAMEO CLIFFS area; the Salt Wash Member, a layered, light-hued sandstone that was deposited by streams, lakes and swamps; and the Brushy Basin Member, a similar deposit that also contains "painted desert" layers, or desert dry-lake deposits that contain mineral-rich volcanic ash. Some of the Brushy Basin Member remains in the CAMEO CLIFFS area in the vicinity of Black Ridge and in the upper levels of the heavily mined hills to the north and south of Utah 46. The other two members top the Entrada Sandstone cliffs almost everywhere within the CAMEO CLIFFS area.

There are "unconformities" between the Navajo and Entrada sandstones, and between the Entrada and Morrison, that is, the deposits were not made in a continuous manner as they now appear in CAMEO CLIFFS. The last deposits of the Navajo and Entrada eroded away over long periods of time before the next permanent deposits began to accumulate.

There are, of course, younger deposits within the area. These are either dune sand held in place by vegetation, active sand dunes, recent water deposits, decomposed rock, rubble fallen from the cliffs, or mixtures of these, all of them products of geologically recent erosion.

Although the region in which CAMEO CLIFFS lies has been subjected to considerable tectonic activity in the past, largely in the form of the upheaval of salt anticlines to the immediate east of the area and the later intrusion of the La Sal Mountains to the north, these violent geologic activities had relatively little effect on the CAMEO CLIFFS area.

The geologic strata in CAMEO CLIFFS North may have been elevated somewhat by the sills and laccoliths -- lava layers intruded between older rock layers -- of the La Sals, but the exposed strata remain relatively level and undisturbed. The geologic strata in CAMEO CLIFFS South are slightly tilted, but were also largely undisturbed by the nearby tectonic activity. This gentle tilting is not obviously related to either the salt anticlines to the east, to the intrusive igneous mountain-forming of the La Sals to the north, or to the northern end of the massive Monument Uplift to the southwest.

The colorful cliffs and canyons of the CAMEO CLIFFS area were exposed in their present form by erosion within the last few million years. This erosion continues today, accelerated by such destructive human activities as mining and grazing.

For a more complete summary of the regional geology surrounding the CAMEO CLIFFS area, refer to the book, *Canyon Country GEOLOGY*.

CAMEO CLIFFS PLANTLIFE

The pinyon-juniper plantlife zone presently dominates the CAMEO CLIFFS area, although there are remnant specimens of trees and other plants from earlier centuries, when the climate of the area was cooler and wetter.

The pinyon-juniper community consists of these hardy trees, plus oak bush, mountain mahogany, Rocky Mountain ash, sage, greasewood, cliffrose, blackbrush, rabbitbush, saltbush, squawbush, Mormon tea, serviceberry, cacti, yucca, snakeweed, desert holly and other less well-known shrubs, plus lichen, cryptogamic soils and a wide variety of native grasses, mosses and annual plants, including an assortment of wildflowers that bloom from early spring to late fall.

Within this general plant community, there are small specialized plant communities, in areas near seeping springs or seasonal and perennial streams, and in sandstone potholes and the wide drywashes that have subsurface water. Each special community harbors its own special types of plantlife, such as reed grasses, horsetails, cattails, algae, ferns, mosses, box elder, cottonwoods and the exotic shrub, tamarisk, as well as a variety of annual plants such as columbine and monkey flower.

Within the CAMEO CLIFFS area, the most conspicuous plantlife remnant of an earlier period of wetter climate is the Ponderosa pine. A few of these stately trees still cling to life on cliffline ledges that are wetted by springs and seepage. The present life zone for these trees is more than a thousand feet higher. Ponderosas can be seen along the northern cliffline of Wilson Point, in a few of the upper drainage lines of Hook and Ladder Draw, and at few other isolated locations.

During the last century, the CAMEO CLIFFS region has been heavily overgrazed by domestic livestock, including sheep, cattle and horses. This has denuded the land of its formerly lush native grasses. That in turn has caused rapid erosion of the soils in the area's canyons, valleys and open meadows, all too often exposing the underlying sandstone and removing rich native soils that took thousands of years to accumulate and stabilize in this relatively arid region.

CAMEO CLIFFS visitors will encounter many examples of this drastic and unnatural erosion while hiking and driving in the area. This erosion is, in turn, destroying the remaining native plant communities by removing the rich soils, causing flash-flooding, lowering water tables and allowing exotic plant species to thrive in the changed environment. The livestock also introduced and spread noxious weeds by carrying their seeds into the area from other regions.

Thus, the domestic livestock industry that leases most of the public land within CAMEO CLIFFS and the surrounding region is directly changing the native plant communities and endangering the native animal species that depend on the plantlife. This in turn is endangering the region's predators -- the foxes, coyotes, badgers, bobcats, eagles, owls, hawks and others -- that use the smaller species for food.

Historic accounts describe the region's canyons and valleys as rich grasslands. Early photographs clearly show this. Most of the grasses presently found in the CAMEO CLIFFS area are non-native species introduced in a vain attempt to slow the obvious erosion -- and to feed still more livestock. Few such exotic grasses thrive for long in the high-desert climate.

The native plantlife and wildlife of CAMEO CLIFFS is in grave danger from the past and continuing abuse of this spectacularly beautiful area of public land.

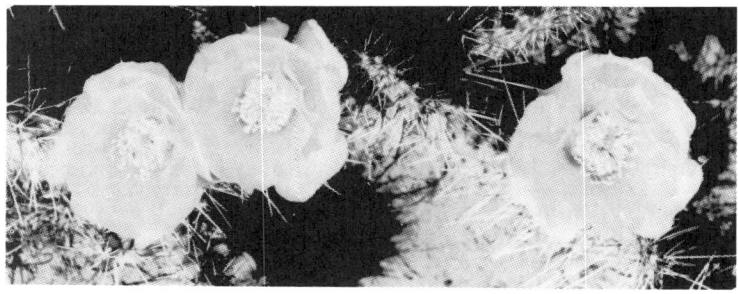

OFF-ROAD VEHICLE TRAIL DESCRIPTION FORMAT

The following headings are used, with minor variations, for describing the off-road vehicle trails within CAMEO CLIFFS. The type of information placed under each heading is noted.

TRAIL NAME The name given the trail by the authors.

ACCESS Instructions for reaching the named trail.

TRAIL LENGTH The total length of the trail, one-way.

TRAIL CONDITIONS Trail surface conditions and grades.

SUGGESTED FOR Vehicles that are suitable for the trail.

DIFFICULTY Difficulty rating for bikers and four-wheelers.

CONNECTIONS Connections to other roads and trails.

SPURS Any spurring trails worth exploring.

DESCRIPTIONS

   BIKING Trail description oriented toward bikers.

   FOUR-WHEELING Trail description for four-wheelers.

   HIKING Suggested hikes from the described vehicle trail.

NOTES Miscellaneous notes about the described trail.

TRAIL DESCRIPTIONS – CAMEO CLIFFS NORTH

PERIMETER AND INTERIOR ROADS

CAMEO CLIFFS North is defined by paved U.S. 191 and Utah 46, and two connected graded roads, Black Ridge Road and Highline Road. It is penetrated by graded Browns Hole Road. All of these roads are shown on the area map on the inside-front cover of this book.

The various off-road vehicle trails that spur from these perimeter and interior roads are described in the following pages, using the description format shown in the sidebar. The graded roads are themselves worth exploring by bikers and four-wheelers and are hence also described.

U.S. 191 AND SPURRING ORV TRAILS

U.S. 191 is the main north-south federal highway within southeastern Utah. It travels between Interstate 70, in east-central Utah, and U.S. 160 in northeastern Arizona. Along the way, it connects the Utah communities of Moab, Monticello, Blanding and Bluff.

As the highway travels between Moab and Monticello, it forms the western boundary of the CAMEO CLIFFS recreation area. Within CAMEO CLIFFS North, Black Ridge Road, Browns Hole Road and Utah 46 spur from U.S. 191, as do the several ORV trails described in the following pages.

Driving U.S. 191 between where it crosses Cane Creek Canyon, and La Sal Junction on farther south, provides an overview of the colorful lower cliffs of CAMEO CLIFFS North. The ORV trails that spur from the highway offer closer looks at the cliffs and some historic remnants, and provide access to some good hiking.

CAMEO CLIFFS North and U.S. 191.

53

TRAIL NAME: CAVE TRAIL

ACCESS: from U.S. 191, at 0.5 and 1.6 miles south of where the highway closely passes the sandstone cliff at the Hole-'n-the-Rock tourist development.

TRAIL LENGTH: about 1.5 miles, plus four 0.3-mile spurs.

TRAIL CONDITIONS: mostly the graded, graveled remnants of a stretch of the original automobile road that was replaced by the present highway, U.S. 191, with four short spurs of packed sediments and sand.

SUGGESTED FOR: four-wheelers, bikers and high-clearance, low-geared highway vehicles, except for the spur, which should not be attempted by any kind of highway vehicle.

DIFFICULTY: easy.

CONNECTIONS: connects at both ends with U.S. 191.

SPURS: four spurs each 0.3 miles long.

Old highway bridge on Cave Trail dated 1933.

DESCRIPTIONS:

BIKING and FOUR-WHEELING:

This short trail is described from its southern end because it is less hazardous to leave the highway at that end. The primary value of this trail is that it is colorfully scenic and that it provides access to several historic remnants plus several short but interesting hikes. After going through the highway fence, 1.6 miles south of the cliff at Hole-'n-the-Rock, the trail travels a stretch of the old highway. The first spur goes right immediately, goes through a good primitive camping area, then ends near the base of an immense, hikable slickrock slope. At mile 0.3, a spur goes right. On this spur, at mile 0.1, stay left and continue for another 0.2 miles, where the spur ends at the base of a sandstone cliff. The large natural cave here has several historic inscriptions in it, as well as other more recent inscriptions and graffiti. The main trail continues beyond the spur to cross a deep ravine over an old stonework-and-concrete bridge that has a benchmark set in its railing that says "*U.S. Coast & Geodetic Survey, elevation 5177.795 above mean sea level, 1933.*" Beyond the bridge, the old road is now somewhat eroded as it skirts through ornate sandstone outcrops and back toward the present highway. At about mile 0.8, a spur goes right at a concrete culvert. This spur ends in a large cliff-alcove in about 0.3 miles. Near its end, the trail leaves the old road to rejoin the main highway. At this point, a spur trail to the right ends in about 0.3 miles on a low sandy bluff facing a beautiful stretch of cliff, where the remnants of an artistic sculpting are still visible at the base of the vertical cliff. This fascinating piece of artwork was created during the 1940s, then later removed at the demand of the Bureau of Land Management. See the sidebar, ALBERT CHRISTENSEN, SANDSTONE SCULPTOR, for more details.

HIKING:

Beyond the end of the southernmost spur trail, hike up onto the slickrock ridge above the trail and continue to its end for a breathtaking view of the vicinity. In addition to climbing up into the cave at the end of the second trail spur, hikers might enjoy exploring the rocky draw above the old bridge, and down the same draw to where it goes beneath the main highway. There is also good free-style slickrock hiking along the base of the northern cliffline in this large alcove, from beyond the end of the northernmost trail spur, and up onto the sandstone dome in the vicinity of the old bridge. It is easy to hike to the remnant sculpting beyond the end of the northernmost spur trail. Look for several short pieces of pipe that are embedded in the slickrock just below the site. The immense grottoes in the cliff to the north of this remnant are exceptionally beautiful.

NOTE: Those who climb into the cave at the end of the short spur trail should take care not to touch or damage any of the historic inscriptions there. Cameras with film fast enough for the indirect lighting in the cave will record the inscriptions without damaging them.

Albert Christensen and his sculpture, above, and what is left of it now, below.

57

TRAIL NAME: MULESHOE CANYON TRAIL

ACCESS: from U.S. 191, immediately north of the highway bridge that crosses the canyon drainage, about 2.6 miles south of Hole-'n-the-Rock.

TRAIL LENGTH: 1.5 miles, one-way.

TRAIL CONDITIONS: eroded graded dirt road for about 0.3 miles, then rocky, eroded packed sediments with occasional sand and rock.

SUGGESTED FOR: four-wheelers and bikers only, although carefully driven high-clearance highway vehicles can safely travel the 0.3-mile old highway stretch.

DIFFICULTY: easy.

CONNECTIONS: none.

SPURS: none.

U.S. 191 crossing Muleshoe Canyon.

DESCRIPTIONS:

BIKING and FOUR-WHEELING:

This short trail is highly scenic as it penetrates the sheer-walled stretch of Muleshoe Canyon to the east of the highway. At mile 0.3, the trail leaves the old highway that it has been traveling. Here, the abutments of the old highway bridge are a few feet from the trail, and traces of the still older wagon road are visible across the canyon just downcanyon from the abutments, angling downward to cross the deep drainage. There is an old corral beside the trail at mile 0.5. The trail crosses the drainage at about 1.0 miles, then again in a few hundred feet at the confluence of Black and Muleshoe canyons. Just beyond this eroded crossing, the trail climbs a short rocky slope, then continues for another few hundred yards, to end at a short sandy loop near the confluence of Muleshoe and an interesting unnamed tributary canyon.

HIKING:

This trail provides some excellent hiking opportunities. From just beyond the second crossing of Muleshoe Creek, hike left up lower Black Canyon. This stretch of that long and rugged drainage is normally dry and easy hiking. At about mile 0.6, there is a pour-off that is difficult to get around. The canyon reaches the first of a series of impassable grotto-pouroffs a few hundred yards on up the canyon, the same natural barriers that block hiking down the drainage from the Benchland Trail.

There are two good hikes from the end of the vehicle trail. One goes up the dry unnamed tributary. To explore this deep canyon, hike up its main drainage as far as possible, then as far as possible up each upper fork of the nearby branch canyon. On the return trip, climb up onto any higher slickrock slopes or terraces that seem interesting. Solstice Arch is about 0.5 miles up the main canyon high on the south side. Angle Arch can best be spotted on the return trip, high in a rock projection near the Muleshoe Canyon confluence on the north side of the main tributary canyon.

From the end of the trail, hike on up Muleshoe Canyon, following the banks of the stream. To do this, it is necessary to change often from one side of the stream to the other, and find paths through the dense streamside vegetation. Continue up the canyon as far as made feasible by the dense growth. There are many small but delightful pools along the way, as well as plentiful signs of wildlife. It is about 2 miles to where the drainage is crossed by the Benchland Trail, at the end of the public stretch of Browns Hole Road.

As an alternate hike in Muleshoe Canyon, park near the old bridge abutments, climb down into the dry drainage and hike downcanyon to where Muleshoe joins Cane Creek Canyon. This stretch of canyon is delightful whenever Muleshoe Creek is flowing, generally in early spring and late fall. It is possible to make this a loop hike by leaving a second vehicle at the Kane Springs Roadside Rest, then hiking down Muleshoe Creek and up Cane Creek to the highway.

Angle Arch on the skyline, above, and Solstice Arch, below.

NOTES:

1. Muleshoe Creek flows intermittently throughout the year, but during the warmer summer months the drainage is generally dry in most of the canyon that this trail penetrates. In the spring, the stream generally flows almost to the highway bridge, then is intermittent on downstream to its confluence with Cane Creek Canyon, to the west of the highway. The stream flows most of the time upcanyon of where this trail ends, to where the canyon is crossed by the Benchland Trail.

2. There is a strange phenomenon in the cliff a few yards back from the end of this vehicle trail. About 60 feet above the trail level a small upward-angling cave contains a large, dark mass of bat guano. This is a fairly common sight, but the old-fashioned pick driven into the mass, and the white rope dangling from the pick, are a mystery, especially since the pick handle seems to be a length of boat oar, rather than the usual shorter hardwood pick-handle. Nor is it easy to conceive how the pick was driven into the mass of guano under the overhanging rock -- or why. The authors of this book would be happy to hear from anyone who can provide an answer to this little mystery.

The confluence of Muleshoe and Black canyons.

The mysterious bat guano cave with dangling rope.

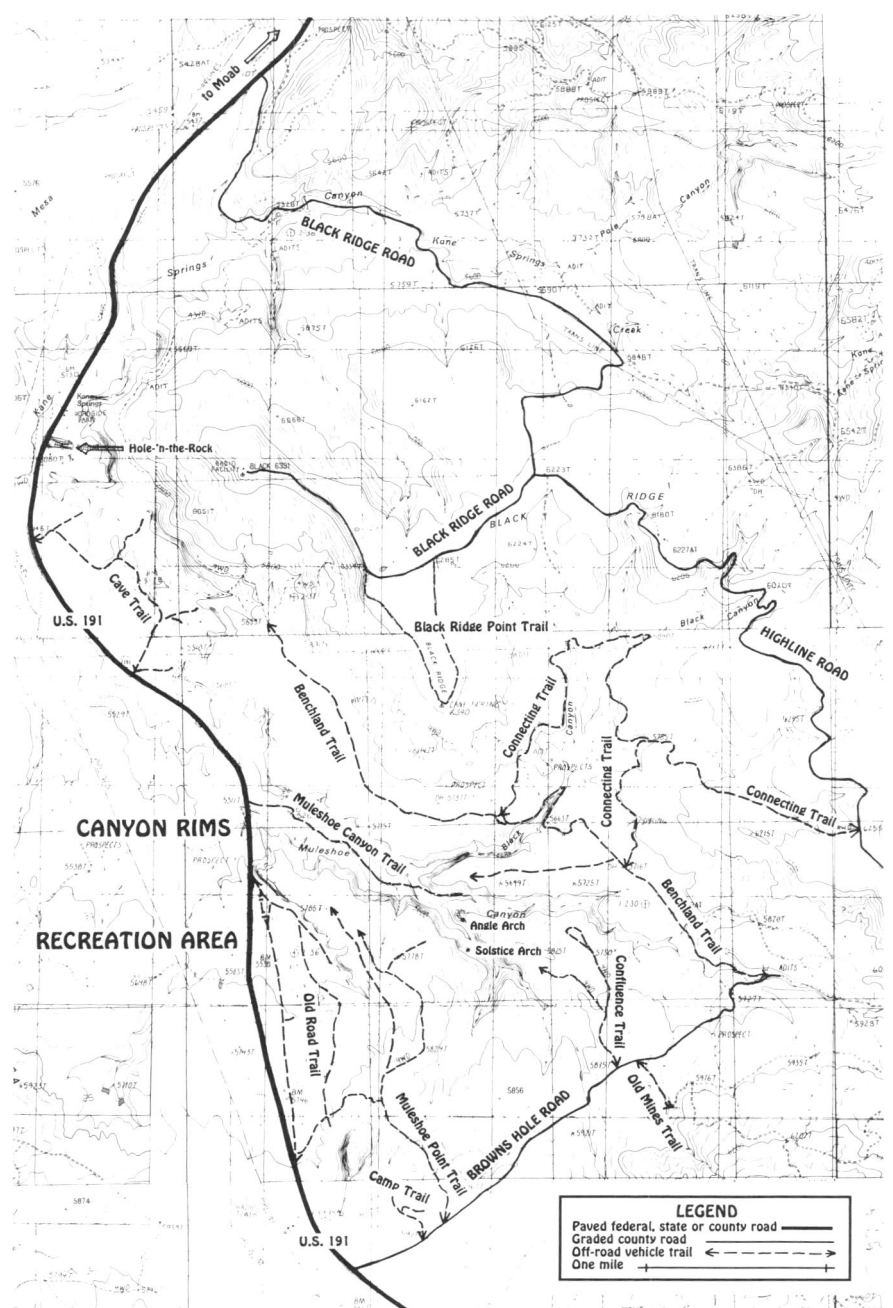

CAMEO CLIFFS North

TRAIL NAME: OLD ROAD TRAIL

ACCESS: from U.S. 191, 3.0 and 4.6 miles south of Hole-'n-the-Rock, or 0.8 miles north of the Browns Hole Road junction, or 0.3 miles north of the industrial plant to the west of the highway in that vicinity.

TRAIL LENGTH: about 1.7 miles on the old road, or 3.0 miles if driven as a loop that includes returning via an ORV trail that goes east of the old road, plus another 0.6 miles for a short dead end spur.

TRAIL CONDITIONS: graded surface on the old road, with several short detours due to erosion, and eroded packed sediments and sand along the ORV trail loop and short spur.

SUGGESTED FOR: four-wheelers and bikers only.

DIFFICULTY: easy.

CONNECTIONS: the trail is a loop from U.S. 191 at both ends, and connects with the Muleshoe Point Trail via a 0.4-mile spur.

SPURS: two short dead end spurs, plus the ORV trail that makes a loop with the old road.

DESCRIPTIONS:

BIKING and FOUR-WHEELING:

This trail is a 1.7-mile stretch of the old graded and graveled road that closely parallels the present paved highway, plus a slightly longer stretch of connecting ORV trail that can be used to make a loop route. This loop is described from its southern end because that is the safest entry from the main highway. This entry is about 4.6 miles south of Hole-'n-the-Rock, or 0.8 miles north of the Browns Hole Road junction. Almost immediately beyond the gate through the highway fence, the ORV trail that makes a return loop trip goes right. The old road continues north. At about mile 0.8 on the old road, watch for a short, steep spur right that goes to an historic water tank built of native rock and concrete. This large tank was probably built in the late 1930s by the CCCs (Civilian Conservation Corps) as a water-development project. It was originally filled by a windmill, which is now gone. Badly bent pieces of its blades are still nearby. At about mile 1.4, the old road has been cut. Here, the trail angles down to the right, crosses a shallow wash, then meets the loop ORV trail. At this junction, the paved highway is about 0.2 miles to the left. The loop ORV trail goes right. From that junction, there is another obscure junction at mile 0.2. The return loop route goes right here across a wash.

The spur straight ahead is dead end. At about 0.2 miles on this spur, a short loop goes left to a primitive camping area. The spur ends a few yards beyond there.

From the noted junction, the return loop route crosses the shallow wash, climbs into higher terrain, then continues generally south, reaching a four-way junction in about 1.0 miles. The trail straight ahead ends shortly. The trail to the left climbs steeply to connect with the Muleshoe Point Trail in about 0.4 miles. The trail right joins the old road in about 0.3 miles, near its southern end, completing the loop route.

HIKING:

There is some good hiking beyond the end of the short dead end spur. Explore the drainage line beyond the end of the trail. Within a few hundred feet, there is a large sandstone alcove in the cliff to the left above the drainage. It is possible to climb on up to the cliff rimlands from either the alcove or via the main drainage, then continue along the rim toward Muleshoe Point, about 1 mile from that point. For a longer loop hike, continue exploring along the rim of Muleshoe Canyon, then return by cutting across the point to the rim access point and back down.

HIKING DIRECTLY FROM U.S. 191

There are two types of hikes that can be taken directly from U.S. 191, without the use of special off-road vehicles. One type is where the distance along a described ORV trail is fairly short to where good hiking begins. The other type is where there is no ORV trail, but good hiking begins directly from the paved highway. Following are some suggestions.

1. **CAVE TRAIL:**

   Park at the pullout at the northern end of this trail, about 0.6 miles south of Hole-'n-the-Rock, then hike the northernmost trail spur to its end and beyond to see the remnant of a sculpting in the cliff there and explore the nearby cliff-alcoves and slickrock expanses. Park beside the southern end of this trail, hike to the cave with its historic inscriptions at the end of the first spur, then hike northwest for a few hundred yards and explore the big ridge of slickrock there beside the main vehicle trail.

2. **MULESHOE CANYON TRAIL:**

   Park at the beginning of this trail, hike the trail into the canyon, then explore each of the upper branches of this canyon as suggested under this trail's description. It is about 1.5 miles to where trail ends and the canyons fork.

3. **DIRECTLY FROM U.S. 191:**

   Park at the pullout east of the highway about 2.0 miles south of Hole-'n-the-Rock and explore along the base of the nearby cliff, then hike southward along the base of the cliff into adjacent Muleshoe Alcove, where a large meander in the sandstone cliffs that wall the highway has formed a gigantic, complex alcove or canyon. Hike up the main drainage of this alcove, then explore as far as possible up each of its various tributaries and along the base of the cliffline as closely as feasible. Next, climb up onto the higher levels of slickrock along the southern part of the alcove to vantage points high above the highway for good views of the alcove and surrounding terrain. From there, it is possible to hike along a high, narrowing terrace almost to the mouth of adjacent Muleshoe Canyon.

Site of the removed Christensen cliff-sculpture.

Hiking Muleshoe Alcove from U.S. 191.

BLACK RIDGE ROAD AND SPURRING ORV TRAILS

Black Ridge Road leaves U.S. 191 about 13 miles south of Moab, at the summit of the Blue Hill grade that ascends out of Moab-Spanish Valley. The graded and graveled road heads east from the highway, then immediately ascends into higher terrain before descending into and traveling up the rugged, dry drainage of upper Cane Creek.

About 3.5 miles from the highway, the road climbs steeply onto Black Ridge, then continues on this high and desolate plateau toward the large microwave tower at its western end. The rimlands beyond and to the north of the tower offer magnificent views of the canyon-slashed terrain below and beyond the lofty point, including Spanish Valley, Behind-the-Rocks, the La Sal Mountains and parts of the northern districts of Canyon Rims Recreation Area. The elevation at the microwave tower is 6391 feet above sea level.

TRAIL NAME: BLACK RIDGE POINT TRAIL

ACCESS FROM: Black Ridge Road, about 1.0 mile from the microwave tower at the end of this road.

TRAIL LENGTH: 1.8-mile loop.

TRAIL CONDITIONS: almost level trail of somewhat rocky but well-packed sediments.

SUGGESTED FOR: bikers, four-wheelers and high-clearance highway vehicles.

DIFFICULTY: easy.

CONNECTIONS: loop trail that joins Black Ridge Road at both ends.

SPURS: none.

DESCRIPTIONS:

BIKING and FOUR-WHEELING:

Back about 1.0 mile from the tower at the end of Black Ridge Road, an easy ORV loop trail closely parallels the rim, heading south onto a projecting tip of Black Ridge that provides spectacular views toward the east, south and west. This 1.8-mile loop is easily passable to bikes and all kinds of off-road vehicles. The leg of the loop that travels near the western rim of Black Ridge can be traveled carefully by high-clearance highway vehicles, which should return the same way.

HIKING:

From where the vehicle trail closely approaches the southern tip of Black Ridge Point, about 0.9 miles from Black Ridge Road, park and walk the few yards to the cliff rim. From along this plateau rim, the sinuous, colorful cliffs and other features of CAMEO CLIFFS North are visible to the south, and many of the geologic features of the northern districts of Canyon Rims Recreation Area spread into the distance to the west. The towering peaks and sweeping lower slopes of the La Sal Mountains dominate the eastern horizon. Far below, parts of the Benchland Trail are visible, winding along the broad terrace that tops the colorful sandstone cliffs along U.S. 191. This high rimland tip offers an almost aerial viewpoint of a breathtaking panorama.

NOTE: The elevation at this viewpoint is 6340 feet above sea level.

HIGHLINE ROAD AND SPURRING ORV TRAILS:

A graded road spurs south about 2.2 miles back from the microwave tower at the end of Black Ridge Road, or about 4.8 miles from U.S. 191 on that road. This is the northern end of the Highline Road. Its southern end connects with Utah 46, about 5.5 miles east of La Sal Junction, on U.S. 191. The road is about 11 miles long. It travels broad benchlands around the base of the La Sal Mountains, occasionally dipping down into and back out of drainage lines. Along the way, numerous undescribed ORV trails spur upward toward the mountains, offering optional exploring for four-wheelers.

The road crosses the Buck Hollow drainage about 3.0 miles from Utah 46. At mile 4.8, the road passes a pool and crosses the small stream that flows down Cottonwood Canyon.

The largest drainage crossed, upper Black Canyon, is near the northern end of the road. There are good views of this rugged canyon from the road as it switchbacks steeply down into, then back out of the narrow gorge.

The broad terraces the road travels offer good views of distant scenic features. The open terrain through which the road goes is either sparsely-vegetated natural mid-elevation meadows, or remnants of pinyon-juniper forest that has been chained, that is, the native trees have been uprooted and killed by dragging heavy anchor chains between huge bulldozers in a usually futile attempt to create better grazing for domestic livestock. The southern stretches of this road are further blighted by a line of steel power-line towers.

Biking through Black Canyon on Highline Road.

The described ORV trail spurs west from the road about 6.2 miles from Utah 46, or about 4.5 miles from its northern end. Another trail spurs from the road about 3 miles from its southern end, where the road crosses Buck Hollow, but this trail enters the private land in Browns Hole and is not described.

Highline Road offers some interesting scenery, and access to one useful spurring ORV trail, but little challenge to four-wheelers. It is a good road for mountain biking, however, especially when traveled from its southern end. Beginning at Utah 46, Highline Road climbs easily for a short distance, then gradually descends for the next 10 miles, until it connects with Black Ridge Road, varying from this long, gentle incline only where the road crosses major drainage lines. Unless bikers return by the same route, a vehicle shuttle is required at either Black Ridge Road or where that road leaves U.S. 191.

Microlake beside Highline Road at Cottonwood Canyon.

TRAIL NAME: CONNECTING TRAIL

ACCESS: from Highline Road, about 4.5 miles from its northern end at Black Ridge Road, or about 6.2 miles from its southern end at Utah 46.

TRAIL LENGTH: 5.6 miles one way, including both legs, or a total of 8.4 miles if traveled as a loop from Highline Road, or 4.6 miles to the Benchland Trail via one leg, or 2.5 miles to that trail via the other leg.

TRAIL CONDITIONS: steep, rough, eroded and rocky many places, with 0.6 miles very rough and eroded along its Black Canyon leg.

SUGGESTED FOR: four-wheelers and more athletic bikers.

DIFFICULTY: easy but rough in places for four-wheelers, moderate to difficult for bikers, with one very difficult stretch on the Black Canyon leg.

CONNECTIONS: connects with the Benchland Trail at its two lower ends, and Highline Road at its upper end.

SPURS: forks into two legs about 1.5 miles from Highland Road.

DESCRIPTIONS:

BIKING:

A challenging loop trip can be taken by biking down this trail from Highline Road, taking the right fork at about 1.5 miles, staying on this Black Canyon leg until it connects with the Benchland Trail in about 3.1 miles, taking that trail south for about 1.3 miles, then ascending 1.0 miles to the fork junction via the trail's other leg and back up to Highland Road. The first leg of this loop is steep and somewhat rough, as it descends the slopes of a picturesque drainage line. At about mile 1.5, the trail forks. The Black Canyon leg descends right to cross a shallow drainage, continues around slopes and still other drainages, then descends to cross mid-Black Canyon about 1.0 miles from the trail fork. Beyond this drainage, the trail is very rough and rocky for about 0.6 miles, with several short steep stretches. It then goes past a uranium mining area. There is a good view of the mined area from a rocky point about 2.2 miles from the trail fork. Beyond the mines, the trail descends steeply to meet the Benchland Trail near a lower stretch of Black Canyon. Go right at this junction to explore this trail to its dead end. Go left to recross Black Canyon and continue on the described loop route. About 1.3 miles from the junction, the other leg of the Connecting Trail turns left from the Benchland Trail, crosses a meadow and ascends rocky slopes and terraces to reach the trail-fork junction in about 1.0 miles. From there, the trail climbs the drainage for 1.5 miles back to Highline Road and the start of the loop route. Bikers should take note that this loop route descends a net 615 feet between Highline Road and the Benchland Trail, then ascends the same amount, plus several sizable climbs and descents along the way.

FOUR-WHEELING:

Four-wheelers can use this trail as a connection between the Benchland Trail and Highline Road, either via its easier short leg or via the more challenging longer leg that goes through the mined area. Four-wheelers can also use the trail as an adventurous loop route as described for bikers.

HIKING:

Hikers can ramble around the abandoned mining areas adjacent to the Black Canyon leg of this trail, and explore the approximately 2 miles of Black Canyon that lies between Highland Road and the Benchland Trail, beginning where that leg of the trail crosses the canyon. The mined stretch of Black Canyon can also be explored by ascending the Black Canyon drainage from where it is crossed by the Benchland Trail. Free-style hiking in the jumbled maze of Morrison Formation strata through which the Connecting Trail travels can also be rewarding.

NOTES:

1. Petrified wood, bone and other collectible rocks are often found in this geologic formation.

2. Do not enter the hazardous mine shafts near this trail.

3. A number of inconspicuous mining trails spur from both legs of the Connecting Trail. Some of these may be worth exploring by adventurous four-wheelers.

Mined area near the Connecting Trail.

BROWNS HOLE ROAD AND SPURRING ORV TRAILS

This graded road leaves U.S. 191 about 5.3 miles south of the Hole-'n-the-Rock tourist development, or about 1.3 miles north of La Sal Junction, and about 0.5 mile south of the pipeline pumping station adjacent to the highway in this vicinity.

The road crosses broad meadows and terraces between a heavily mined hill to the south and a series of developing canyons to the north. The public part of the road, which is also designated San Juan County 130, ends where it reaches the upper drainage of Muleshoe Canyon and enters the private land of Browns Hole.

The road on into Browns Hole beyond a posted gate is private and should not be used by recreationists.

The primary value of Browns Hole Road is for access to the several off-road vehicle trails that branch from its 3-mile length, although the road does offer good scenic views of immense sandstone domes, the rugged, heavily-prospected hill to the south, and the more distant La Sal Mountains, plus occasional glimpses of the rugged, rocky drainages to the north of the road.

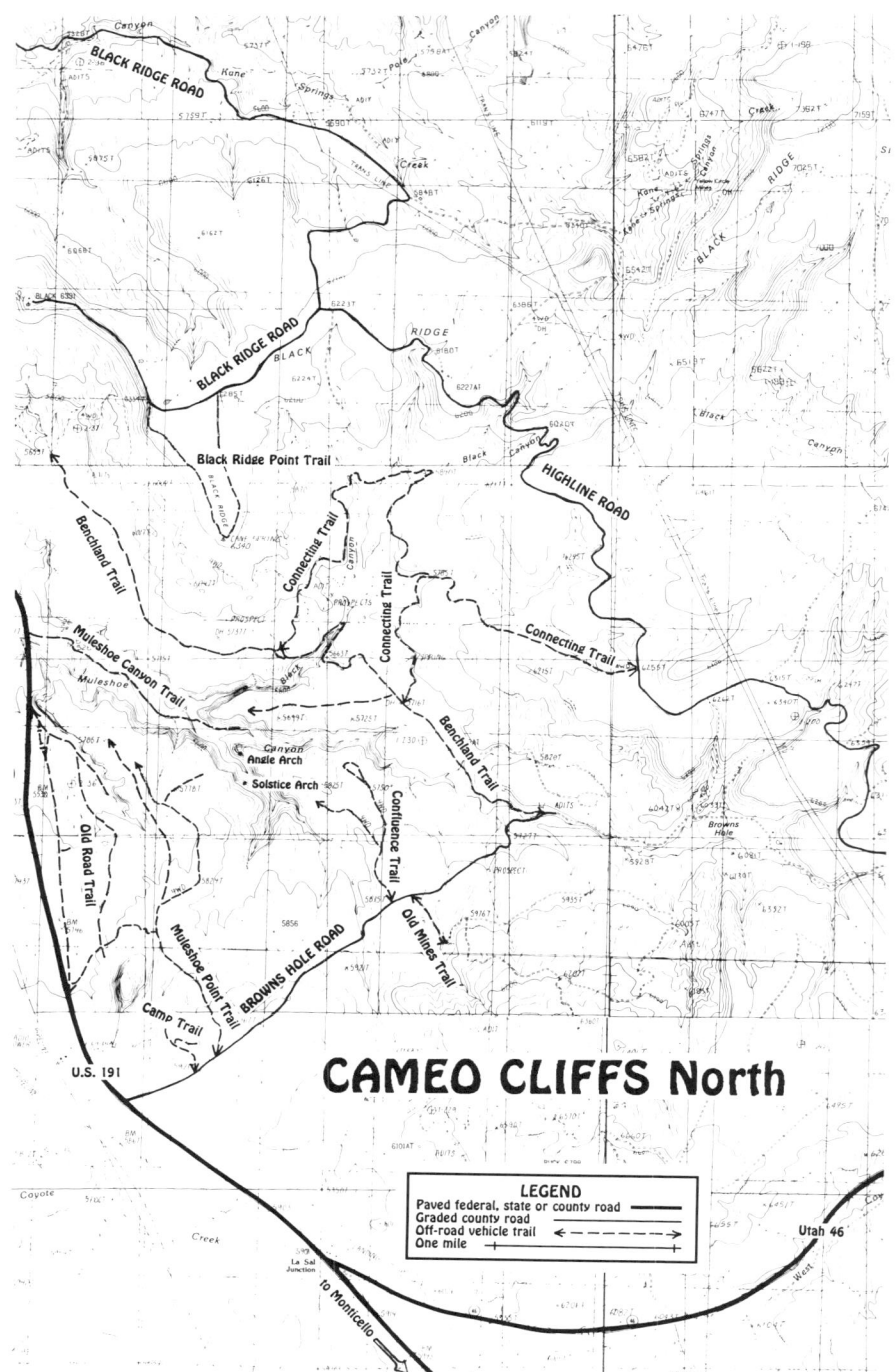

TRAIL NAME: CAMP TRAIL

ACCESS: from Browns Hole Road, about 0.45 miles from U.S. 191.

TRAIL LENGTH: 0.4 miles, one way, plus a short spur.

TRAIL CONDITIONS: packed sediments, slickrock and soft sand, with mostly slickrock on its short spur.

SUGGESTED FOR: four-wheelers and bikers, plus high-clearance highway vehicles when the sand is not too dry.

DIFFICULTY: easy, except when the sand near the end of the trail is very dry.

CONNECTIONS: none.

SPURS: one short spur near the end of the trail.

Hiking toward The Nipples from the end of Camp Trail.

DESCRIPTIONS:

BIKING and FOUR-WHEELING:

The main use of this trail by vehicles is for the good primitive camping sites it offers and for hiking access to the nearby sandstone buttes. The short spur trail that goes to the right at about 0.25 miles climbs onto a low sandstone mesa, which offers more good camping and a panoramic view of the La Sal Mountains and nearby geologic features.

HIKING:

From the end of this trail or its spur, hike up onto the adjacent sandstone butte. The two large suggestive tips on top of the southern butte that are visible from the main highway are known as "The Nipples." They were a familiar landmark along an historic cattle-drive route that closely paralleled the present federal highway. It is easy to attain the top of this butte, with its full-circle panoramic view.

Weathered historic inscriptions on one of The Nipples.

TRAIL NAME: MULESHOE POINT TRAIL

ACCESS: from Browns Hole Road, about 0.6 miles from U.S. 191.

TRAIL LENGTH: 2.2 miles one way on the main trail, plus 0.8 miles one way on a spur trail.

TRAIL CONDITIONS: largely somewhat eroded packed sediments, with sand and rock in a few places.

SUGGESTED FOR: four-wheelers and bikers only.

DIFFICULTY: easy.

CONNECTIONS: connects with the Old Road Trail.

SPURS: has one spur about 0.8 mile long, with a short spur off of that.

DESCRIPTIONS:

BIKING and FOUR-WHEELING:

This trail and its spurs offer little for bikers and four-wheelers except good distant views of the La Sal Mountains, nearby canyons and some of the lowlands to the west of the main trail. The main value of the trail and its spurs is for access to some good hiking. At about mile 0.9 from Browns Hole Road, an inconspicuous trail to the left descends steeply to join the Old Road Trail in the lower terrain to the west in about 0.5 miles. The main trail reaches a junction at about mile 1.1. The main trail goes left here, while a spur almost as long continues ahead. The main trail as described travels closely parallel to the western rim of this elevated area, then ends 1.0 miles beyond the junction near a rocky outcropping.

The spur that went straight ahead at mile 1.1 forks again in another 0.6 miles. The spur that continues left ends within a few hundred yards on a rocky ridge. The spur right ends at the base of a low sandstone mesa in a few hundred yards.

HIKING:

For the best hiking from this trail, hike, drive or ride to the end of the main trail, or to the left end of the spur trail described above, then continue hiking out onto Muleshoe Point, high above picturesque Muleshoe Canyon, staying somewhat higher than the canyon rim, past some oddly-shaped sandstone towers. From the point, where Muleshoe Canyon and the main highway are visible below, explore the strangely eroded sandstone pinnacles and fins along the western cliff-rim, then return to the vehicle trail.

For an alternate route, drive or ride to the end of the right fork of the spur trail, climb up onto the low sandstone mesa, cross it to the rim of Muleshoe Canyon, then hike in either direction along the rim. In the downcanyon direction, the rim is soon cut by a short tributary drainage. There is a seasonally-active hawk nest perched on a ledge in the opposite rim of this short canyon. The hike along the upcanyon rim, as it skirts around the rims of various tributary canyons, can be as long as desired, or until Muleshoe Canyon reaches the junction of Browns Hole Road and the Benchland Trail.

U.S. 191 and Behind-the-Rocks from Muleshoe Point.

TRAIL NAME: CONFLUENCE TRAIL

ACCESS: from Browns Hole Road, about 2.0 miles from U.S. 191.

TRAIL LENGTH: 1.0 miles, one way, with a 0.5-mile one-way spur.

TRAIL CONDITIONS: packed sediments, with some rock and sand, and quite eroded in places, especially on the spur.

SUGGESTED FOR: four-wheelers and bikers only.

DIFFICULTY: easy.

CONNECTIONS: none.

SPURS: one 0.5-mile spur.

DESCRIPTIONS:

    BIKING and FOUR-WHEELING:

This trail and its spur offer little for bikers and four-wheelers except good distant views of the La Sal Mountains and glimpses of nearby canyons. The main value of the trail and its spur is for access to some good hiking. The trail leaves Browns Hole Road about 2.0 miles from U.S. 191, then travels across open brushy terrain. At mile 0.3, the 0.5-mile spur goes left. At mile 0.6 continue straight ahead. At mile 0.7 the trail begins a very rough and rocky loop 0.6 miles long, or 0.3 miles to its tip.

The spur that goes left at mile 0.3 ends in 0.5 miles below a higher mesa and just above the rim of a short but ruggedly picturesque tributary of Muleshoe Canyon.

HIKING:

From the end of the main trail, hike the rim of Muleshoe Canyon in either direction. In the downcanyon direction, the confluence of Muleshoe Canyon and a short but spectacular unnamed tributary is about 0.7 miles beyond the end of the trail. The hike to this photogenic confluence is more picturesque along the rim of the tributary canyon. This hike begins at the end of the described spur. Solstice Arch can be seen in the far canyon wall at one point, but is difficult to spot unless sunlight is passing through its opening. This happens only during the peak of the summer around noon, hence its name. There are masses of colorful agate along the canyon rimlands and on the point of land above their confluence.

Muleshoe Canyon from above its confluence with Black Canyon.

TRAIL NAME: OLD MINES TRAIL

ACCESS: from Browns Hole Road, about 2.1 miles from U.S. 191.

TRAIL LENGTH: 0.3 miles, more for intrepid mine-trail explorers.

TRAIL CONDITIONS: somewhat eroded graded dirt road.

SUGGESTED FOR: all kinds of vehicles, to the first mines.

DIFFICULTY: easy.

CONNECTIONS: none.

SPURS: continues beyond the described mines into a maze of eroded undescribed mining trails on the large hill of Morrison Formation deposits that dominates the southern end of CAMEO CLIFFS North, between Browns Hole Road and Utah 46.

Remains of an old military vehicle at the mine site.

DESCRIPTIONS:

BIKING and FOUR-WHEELING:

This short trail has little value except as access to an interesting mining area that has several shafts, two dugout structures, the remains of several old vehicles and assorted machinery and junk left behind when the mining ended several decades ago.

HIKING: none.

NOTE: Do not enter the old mine shafts at this or any other uranium mining site in the region. There is always some danger of rock collapse, but the greatest danger is from accumulations of invisible radon gas. Inhalation of this radioactive gas can cause severe health problems years later. Other, possibly hazardous chemical odors have been detected in the vicinity of these mine shafts.

One of the two dugout dwellings at the mine site.

TRAIL NAME: BENCHLAND TRAIL

ACCESS: from Browns Hole Road, about 3.1 miles from U.S. 191.

TRAIL LENGTH: about 4.5 miles, one way.

TRAIL CONDITIONS: packed sediments, largely level, with occasional rough stretches and eroded places, with the hazard of domestic cattle in the area during the spring months.

SUGGESTED FOR: four-wheelers, bikers and carefully driven low-geared, high-clearance highway vehicles.

DIFFICULTY: easy.

CONNECTIONS: connects with the two legs of the Connecting Trail that connect the Benchland Trail with Highland Road.

SPURS: has one spur that is 0.9 miles long.

DESCRIPTIONS:

BIKING and FOUR-WHEELING:

This trail leaves Browns Hole Road about 3.1 miles from U.S. 191, then travels a relatively level benchland below broken terraces of Morrison Formation sandstone at an intermediate level between U.S. 101 and Highland Road. At mile 0.8, a highly eroded mine trail branches right. At mile 1.1, the shorter leg of the Connecting Trail spurs right. At mile 1.2, a 0.9-mile spur goes left, to end a few hundred yards from the tip of the high peninsula between Muleshoe and Black canyons. At mile 1.3, a short spur to the right ends at a spring-fed pool at the base of a low bluff. This spring and its surrounding vegetation are heavily trampled by cattle.

At about mile 1.8, the trail reaches a viewpoint overlooking a deep, narrow grotto of Black Canyon, then skirts around that part of the drainage. At about mile 2.3, there is a crude rock-and-log corral in the sandstone wall to the right of the trail. At about mile 2.4, the longer leg of the Connecting Trail spurs right. Beyond this junction, the Benchland Trail continues for about another 2.0 miles, to end at a steep eroded stretch. The trail actually continues to a series of old mining sites, but is blocked to all vehicle travel by a fence just beyond the steep descent. The blocked trail travels high above the big alcove that is traveled by Cave Trail, and below the microwave tower at the end of Black Ridge Road.

HIKING:

There are several good places to hike from this trail. The spur that leaves the main trail at mile 1.2 goes toward the confluence of Muleshoe and Black canyons. Hiking either canyon rim from the end of this spur to the lofty viewpoint above that confluence, then back via the other rim, provides many excellent views of these two deep, sheer-walled canyons. The view from above the confluence on down the canyon toward the main highway and beyond, is highly picturesque.

From where the main trail crosses the Black Canyon drainage, a short hike upstream leads to the mining area described under the Connecting Trail. A short hike down the drainage ends where a series of impassably deep and narrow grottoes have been carved into solid rock by flooding water. It is possible to hike on downcanyon for a short distance by climbing out of the drainage and continuing at a level high above the spectacular grottoes.

Hiking for a mile or so beyond the end of the described main trail affords good views of the lower terrain to the west.

Skirting around Black Canyon on the Benchland Trail.

OFF-ROAD VEHICLE TRAIL DESCRIPTION FORMAT

The following headings are used, with minor variations, for describing the off-road vehicle trails within CAMEO CLIFFS. The type of information placed under each heading is noted.

TRAIL NAME The name given the trail by the authors.

ACCESS Instructions for reaching the named trail.

TRAIL LENGTH The total length of the trail, one-way.

TRAIL CONDITIONS Trail surface conditions and grades.

SUGGESTED FOR Vehicles that are suitable for the trail.

DIFFICULTY Difficulty rating for bikers and four-wheelers.

CONNECTIONS Connections to other roads and trails.

SPURS Any spurring trails worth exploring.

DESCRIPTIONS

    BIKING Trail description oriented toward bikers.

    FOUR-WHEELING Trail description for four-wheelers.

    HIKING Suggested hikes from the described vehicle trail.

NOTES Miscellaneous notes about the described trail.

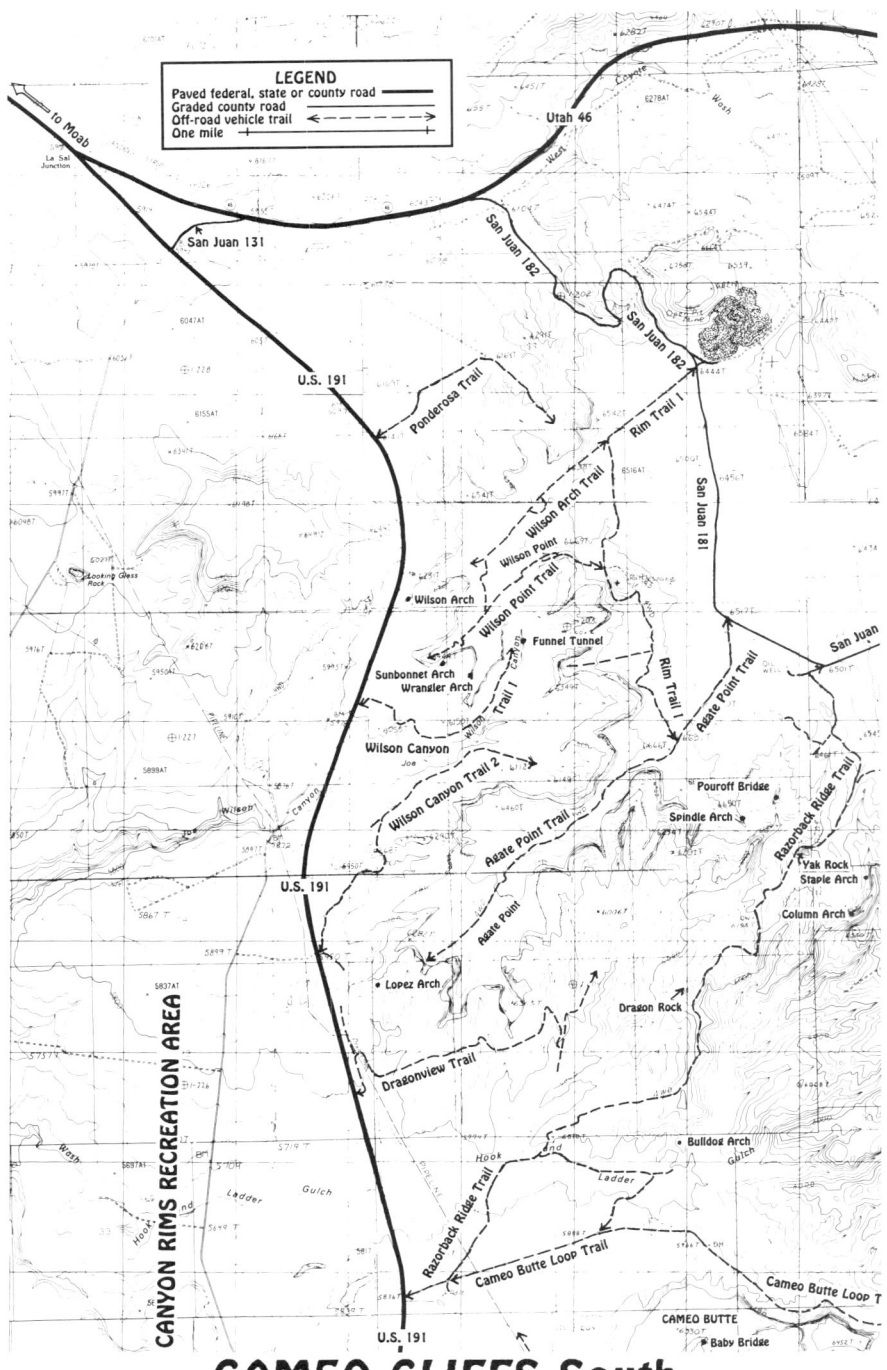

TRAIL DESCRIPTIONS – CAMEO CLIFFS SOUTH

PERIMETER AND INTERIOR ROADS

CAMEO CLIFFS South is defined by paved U.S. 191, Utah 46, San Juan 114, San Juan 370, San Juan 116 and an off-road vehicle trail. It is penetrated by San Juan 131, San Juan 181 and San Juan 182. All of these roads and the defining off-road vehicle trail are shown on the area map on the inside-back cover of this book.

The various off-road vehicle trails that spur from these perimeter and interior roads are described in the following pages, using the description format shown in the sidebar.

U.S. 191 AND SPURRING ORV TRAILS

U.S. 191 is the main north-south federal highway within southeastern Utah. It travels between Interstate 70, in east-central Utah, and U.S. 160 in northeastern Arizona. Along the way, it connects the Utah communities of Moab, Monticello, Blanding and Bluff.

As the highway travels between Moab and Monticello, it forms the western boundary of the CAMEO CLIFFS recreation area. Within CAMEO CLIFFS South, Utah 46, San Juan 131 and San Juan 114 spur from U.S. 191, as do the several ORV trails described in the following pages.

Within CAMEO CLIFFS, San Juan 131 is a short piece of an old road that is an eastern extension of the Hatch Wash Road that travels southwest from U.S. 191 into Canyon Rims Recreation Area. This short cutoff road between U.S. 191 and Utah 46 can be traveled by any vehicle. Where it crosses West Coyote Creek, on an exposure of sandstone about midway, there are some interesting grottoes cut into the rock and a curious small dugout nearby. There is usually flowing water in the creek there.

Driving U.S. 191 between Utah 46 and San Juan 114 provides an overview of the colorful lower cliffs of CAMEO CLIFFS South. The ORV trails that spur from the highway offer more intimate looks at the cliffs and two intricate canyon systems, and provide access to some outstanding hiking. Some hiking is available from the highway itself.

89

*Tim Martin flying through Wilson Arch.
Photo by Darla Martin.*

Wilson Arch from the end of the Wilson Point Trail.

TRAIL NAME: PONDEROSA TRAIL

ACCESS: from U.S. 191, about 2.4 miles south of La Sal Junction, where Utah 46 goes east.

TRAIL LENGTH: about 1.2 miles, one way.

TRAIL CONDITIONS: eroded packed sediments, with a little sand.

SUGGESTED FOR: four-wheelers and bikers only, for more than a few yards beyond the highway fenceline.

DIFFICULTY: easy.

CONNECTIONS: none.

SPURS: none.

DESCRIPTIONS:

    BIKING and FOUR-WHEELING:

    This trail is of little value to four-wheelers and bikers except as access to some interesting hiking. The trail heads northeast from the main highway, paralleling the northern cliffline of Wilson Point, for about 1.0 miles, then angles right to enter and end in a large cliff-walled alcove.

    HIKING:

    For some interesting hiking, park just beyond the gate in the highway fence. Any vehicle can go this far. Hike along the fenceline toward the cliff, then along its base through two large seep-caves, with their rows of mosses and delicate columbine, then around the sandstone point into the next much larger alcove with its own even larger seep-cave. Those with appropriate vehicles can drive to the end of the trail and explore the second large alcove there.

NOTE: Both alcoves have remnant Ponderosa pines growing on their upper terraces, and both present good examples of the greatly accelerated soil erosion caused by the overgrazing that has destroyed the native moisture-holding grasses.

CAMEO CLIFFS ROCKHOUNDING

Rockhounding in the CAMEO CLIFFS area is much like that in most of canyon country. It consists of knowing what types of mineral specimens exist in the various geologic strata there, then seeking readily available exposures of these strata.

As noted in the sidebar on CAMEO CLIFFS geology, there are only three geologic strata there, the Morrison Formation, Entrada Sandstone and Navajo Sandstone. The Morrison Formation has three members. All three are found in CAMEO CLIFFS. Entrada Sandstone also has three members, but only two of these exist in CAMEO CLIFFS. Following is a summary of what these geologic strata have to offer rockhounds and casual collectors of mineral specimens.

MORRISON FORMATION. The uppermost members of this formation contain a wide variety of specimens, including agate, chert, petrified wood and bone, plant and invertebrate fossils, calcite, barite, geodes, celestite, selenite, gastroliths, coprolite and dinosaur tracks. Since the CAMEO CLIFFS area has not in the past been used much for recreational rockhounding, there are no proven sites for finding such specimens, but several of the area's roads and ORV trails travel through the Morrison. In CAMEO CLIFFS North these are the Black Ridge Road, Highline Road, and the Benchland and Connecting ORV trails, with some minor exposures along several other trails. In CAMEO CLIFFS South, Utah 46, San Juan 182, and the Wilson Arch Trail and Rim Trail I go through exposures of Morrison. The heavily prospected hills in both areas of CAMEO CLIFFS are of the same formation.

The lowest member of the Morrison, the Tidwell Member, tops the colorful bluffs of CAMEO CLIFFS. The softer, dark red deposits of this member contain enormous quantities of colorful agate in this area. As the softer sediments of this member erode away, the harder agate remains on the surface at that level, or tumbles down the cliff to lower levels. The exposed agate nodules range in size from small chips to enormous masses weighing several tons. One agate boulder at least eight feet in diameter was observed by the authors at the base of a cliff, still intact after it had fallen several hundred feet. To collect agate, rockhounds need only reach the base or rim of any Entrada Sandstone cliff in the CAMEO CLIFFS area. Many exposures of this red-hued rock some distance from the cliffs still have remnants of weather-resistant agate lying around on their surfaces. Some of the ORV trail descriptions call attention to large exposures of agate, and CAMEO CLIFFS hikers will encounter this colorful semi-precious gem rock almost everywhere they explore. Agate Point was named after its abundant mineral, but the rimlands of the other elevated peninsulas in the area are also rich in agate.

ENTRADA SANDSTONE. The two members of this colorful sandstone that exist in the CAMEO CLIFFS area rarely have mineral specimens in them, but special kinds of agate do occur in the Dewey Bridge Member in some canyon country locations. If any occurs in CAMEO CLIFFS, it is obscured by the massive amounts of agate that fall everywhere from the lowest member of the Morrison Formation. The Entrada Slickrock member has no known mineral specimens, but does offer delightfully intriguing patterns of color -- subtle shades of cameo pink and white -- that defy explanation. These colorful exhibits can only be collected by photography.

NAVAJO SANDSTONE. This white sandstone, that serves as a foundation for the other geologic strata in CAMEO CLIFFS, also offers few collectible mineral specimens, although during their explorations the authors did find one specimen of petrified wood in mid-Navajo. In other parts of the canyon country region, numerous sites of petrified trees and other vegetation, as well as the petrified tracks of dinosaurs and other ancient animals, have been found by the authors and others in the sediments of former playa lakes within the desert-dune deposits of Navajo Sandstone. The authors found one track site in CAMEO CLIFFS while exploring a remote area on foot, so there is a chance still more exist, waiting for some observant rockhound or hiker to discover.

TRAIL NAME: WILSON CANYON TRAIL 1

ACCESS: from U.S. 191 about 0.6 miles south of Wilson Arch.

TRAIL LENGTH: about 1.3 miles, one way, with an additional 0.3 miles of wheel tracks that are difficult to travel.

TRAIL CONDITIONS: eroded packed sediments, some rock and a little sand, on the described trail.

SUGGESTED FOR: four-wheelers and bikers only.

DIFFICULTY: easy, on the described trail.

CONNECTIONS: none.

SPURS: none.

Upper Joe Wilson Canyon.

DESCRIPTIONS:

BIKING and FOUR-WHEELING:

This short trail provides close views of the large alcove in the colorful Entrada Sandstone cliffs formed by the upper drainages of Joe Wilson Canyon. From U.S. 191, the trail descends to cross one tributary drainage, then swings around open slopes and meadows toward the southern tip of Wilson Point. Along this first stretch, two arches are visible in the cliffs. Sunbonnet Arch is a relatively small opening through a large arc of rock near the cliff top north of the trail. Wrangler Arch is the large arching mass of sandstone in the center of the wall of rock that faces west. Its large opening is not apparent from the trail, but around noon in mid-summer, sunlight through its opening shows on the rock slope below the span.

Beyond where the arches are visible, the trail travels around an elongated fin of red sandstone, then reaches the cliff. From there, it travels between the cliff and the main upper drainage of Joe Wilson Canyon, ending at mile 1.3 at an easy turn-around. A very rough set of wheel tracks continues for another 0.3 miles, but is not recommended.

HIKING:

This trail offers access to some good hiking. For the first hike, park near the low ridge that separates the elongated fin of sandstone from the main cliffline, then hike up through that gap toward Wrangler and Sunbonnet arches. The remnants of an old *"rip-gut"* fence cross that gap. The surprisingly large size of Wrangler's opening can be seen and photographed from directly below the span.

From this same vicinity, find a way down into Joe Wilson Canyon, then hike as far as possible up the main drainage. A fairly deep pool of water generally prevents getting all the way to Funnel Tunnel, a curiously-shaped natural opening at the base of the deep and narrow grottoes at the end of the canyon. To reach the four-foot opening, either wade the cold water, or return in the winter and walk its frozen surface. For a canyon-rim view of Funnel Tunnel, hike beyond the end of the described trail and around the grottoes at the canyon head to the other side, where the span and "funnel" behind it are visible about 40 feet below.

For still more hiking, follow the sandstone cliff wall beyond the end of the trail, exploring the several seep-caves and slickrock slopes and terraces along the way, to at least as far as the first gigantic fin of sandstone that projects from the cliffs into the broad alcove. The entire Joe Wilson Canyon alcove can be explored from the end of this trail, but beyond the noted fin, the cliffline and the interesting tributary drainages of the canyon are more easily reached from Wilson Canyon Trail 2.

NOTE: A *"rip-gut"* fence is a barrier to cattle constructed from dead juniper trees. The sharp-limbed trees are placed in a tangle too dense for cattle to penetrate without "ripping their guts" on the sharp limbs. The remnants of such crude but effective fences, built entirely of local available materials, are found throughout the region.

"Rip-gut" fence, near Wilson Canyon Trail 1.

Upper Joe Wilson Canyon.

THE ARCHES AND BRIDGES OF CAMEO CLIFFS

Entrada and Navajo sandstones readily form natural arches and bridges wherever they are exposed in the canyon country region, including the CAMEO CLIFFS recreation area.

There are a few small arches in the backcountry of CAMEO CLIFFS North, but more, a couple quite large, in CAMEO CLIFFS South. Most of the arches are in Entrada Sandstone, but three are in the Navajo Sandstone.

There are two known and named arches visible from U.S. 191. These are large and beautiful Wilson Arch, once known as "Window Arch," and Lopez Arch, a young but lovely span farther south, whose small opening will enlarge with time. Wilson Arch is beside the highway about 3.5 miles south of Crescent Junction, where Utah 46 heads east. Lopez Arch is visible several hundred feet east of the highway, about 2.3 miles south of Wilson Arch.

During our explorations of the CAMEO CLIFFS area in 1991, we found and documented 11 additional arches of significant size, plus a number of smaller openings that we did not consider significant. Our definition of "significant" was not based on size alone, but included such factors as method of formation, location, chance of getting larger with time, and aesthetics. Thus, a few of the arches we considered to be significant enough to deserve names and documentation had fairly small openings, but had other redeeming features.

Wilson Arch and Lopez Arch were already named, and their names have appeared in print. Since we could find no record of names for the other arches we found, we gave them names for the purpose of discussing them in this book. These assigned names are "official" only in that they are probably the scholastically-recognized "first in print."

The locations of most of the arches we named appear in the various off-road trail descriptions in this book, but are summarized here for the sake of those who enjoy "collecting" arches. Photographs of some of these arches appear in this book. Spindle Arch appears on its front cover.

Following are the names, approximate sizes and locations of the 12 arches we named. For more precise locations, refer to the appropriate area maps. For more precise measurements, feel free to measure them.

CAMEO CLIFFS North

NAME	OPENING SIZE	LOCATION	ROCK
Angle Arch	opening under 10 feet	Muleshoe Canyon	Entrada
Solstice Arch	opening under 10 feet	Muleshoe Canyon	Entrada

CAMEO CLIFFS South

NAME	OPENINGS	LOCATION	ROCK
Sunbonnet Arch	opening under 10 feet	Wilson Point	Entrada
Wrangler Arch	about 8 by 30 feet	Wilson Point	Entrada
Funnel Tunnel	opening under 10 feet	Joe Wilson Canyon	Navajo
Spindle Arch	opening under 10 feet	Agate Point	Entrada
Pouroff Bridge	opening under 10 feet	Hook & Ladder Dr	Navajo
Staple Arch	opening under 10 feet	Hook & Ladder Dr	Entrada
Column Arch	opening under 10 feet	Hook & Ladder Dr	Navajo
Bulldog Arch	openings under 10 feet	Hook & Ladder Dr	Entrada
One-Eye Window	4-1/2 by 30 feet	Cameo Butte	Entrada
Baby Bridge	opening under 10 feet	Cameo Butte	Entrada

Those who wish to know more about canyon country's numerous natural arches and bridges should refer to the book, *Canyon Country* ARCHES & BRIDGES.

The Authors

Wrangler Arch, Joe Wilson Canyon.

TRAIL NAME: WILSON CANYON TRAIL 2

ACCESS: from U.S. 191, about 2.0 miles south of Wilson Arch.

TRAIL LENGTH: about 2.0 miles, one way, plus a very short optional spur.

TRAIL CONDITIONS: eroded packed sediments, some sand and a little slickrock, with part of the trail obscured by seasonal vegetation in the summer and fall.

SUGGESTED FOR: four-wheelers and bikers only.

DIFFICULTY: easy, but with a few places rutted by erosion.

CONNECTIONS: none.

SPURS: one very short spur at the trail's beginning.

DESCRIPTIONS:

BIKING and FOUR-WHEELING:

This trail provides access into the southern part of the huge cliff-alcove formed by upper Joe Wilson Canyon, offering alternate views of this spectacular, red-walled amphitheater and easy access to more outstanding hiking. Within a few yards of going through the highway fence about 2.0 miles south of Wilson Arch, a short spur goes right to end in a few yards among the sparse trees on top of a ridge of dune sand. The only use of this spur is for access to some good slickrock hiking.

The main trail angles northward toward the tip of a long ridge of red-hued sandstone. It dips down to cross a drainage, reaches the ridge at about mile 0.6, then ascends steeply across the lower end of the ridge in order to continue. Where the trail reaches the dune sand just beyond the ridge, the trail is generally obscured by seasonal vegetation, but it crosses the meadow there in a generally northeasterly direction for about 0.2 miles then swings more easterly. All vehicles should attempt to find and stay on the existing wheel tracks through this short stretch in order to prevent creating still more confusion.

Beyond the meadow, the trail is clear as it penetrates the gigantic alcove created by upper Joe Wilson Canyon, traveling fairly close to and parallel to its main drainage. For its last few hundred feet, the trail angles east and drops down into lower terrain, to end at about mile 2.0 on the slickrock floor of a tributary drainage. At one time, the trail continued into a maze of spurring mineral-search trails, but the land is slowly recovering from this mindless onslaught of destruction and the remnant trails should not be driven by four-wheelers or ridden by bikers.

HIKING:

As with most of the shorter vehicle trails in CAMEO CLIFFS, this trail provides better opportunities for hiking than for four-wheeling. At the end of the short spur at the beginning of the trail, one good route goes along the slickrock canyon rim toward Lopez Pocket, a deep slash in the main cliffline, with some lateral explorations into higher levels of the slickrock slopes along the way. It is possible to go almost to the end of this deep cut, but difficult to drop down into the drainage there. Farther back along the rim, it is practical to drop down into and cross the drainage, then ascend the steep opposite slope to its summit. From there it is easy to explore further. This slickrock ridge ends above Lopez Arch, with its relatively small opening but beautiful arching span of smoothly eroded sandstone. See the sidebar, LOPEZ ARCH.

Lopez Arch.

From the same starting point, it is possible to get to below Lopez Arch by descending into the drainage by either of two routes, one upcanyon from the spur trail end, the other downcanyon, then hiking down the drainage and around the slickrock base and up to the arch.

Two other short hikes begin at about mile 0.6 on the main trail, where it crosses the tongue of sandstone. There, it is easy to ascend the sandstone ridge to the base of the higher cliff and an excellent viewpoint, or hike up the south side of the ridge on its lower slickrock slopes to the end of the drainage.

From the end of the main trail, there are several fairly short but interesting hikes. One goes down the white sandstone tributary drainage to the main Joe Wilson Canyon drainage, then explores that and still another upper tributary. These drainages have cut into the top of the white Navajo Sandstone. In the tributaries, erosion from flowing water has formed many ornate potholes and small grottoes.

Another route from the trail end ascends the nearby slickrock slopes to the higher levels behind massive Owl Rock and the sandstone tower behind it, then explores the sandstone terraces beyond and above these towering monoliths. Still another route goes to the left of these prominences, generally following the canyon walls wherever possible, into the several large seep-caves, along the base of the large sandstone fin to the north, then either continuing into the northern part of the canyon or returning via the drainages.

Owl Rock and nearby tower, from Agate Point.

NOTES:

1. Owl Rock and the tower behind it seem to be weather-magnets of some sort. The first time we, the authors of this book, climbed the heights behind them, in the late spring of 1991, the weather was delightful when we ascended, but we were soon chased out by a heavy snow flurry. The second time, in August of the same year, the sky was sunny when we ascended, but quickly turned ominous, with great black masses of lightning-riven clouds bearing down on us. This was all highly photogenic but more than a little strange!

2. The first 0.5 miles of this trail from U.S. 191 cross undeveloped private land but, since the trail is an access route into a large area of public land, it should remain open to public travel. If the highway gate should be locked, or the trail otherwise closed to public travel, this should be reported to the nearest BLM office.

Late spring snow at Owl Rock.   See page 102 for the later storm.

TRAIL NAME: DRAGONVIEW TRAIL

ACCESS: from U.S. 191 about 2.8 miles south of Wilson Arch or about 2.0 miles north of that highway's junction with paved San Juan 114.

TRAIL LENGTH: about 2.4 miles, one way.

TRAIL CONDITIONS: eroded packed sediments, sand, rough rock and slickrock, with one very steep stretch and part of the trail obscured by seasonal vegetation.

SUGGESTED FOR: four-wheelers and bikers only.

DIFFICULTY: easy for four-wheelers, except for a short moderate stretch, but difficult for bikers.

CONNECTIONS: none.

SPURS: one short spur near the trail start.

DESCRIPTIONS:

BIKING:

Bikers will find traveling this trail quite demanding due to soft wash sand, several short but steep grades, rocks in the trail and the very rough descent into the wash bottom near the end of the trail. Those who enjoy such challenges will find this trail rewarding from both its variety and its spectacular views of the complex upper drainages of Hook and Ladder Gulch. At about mile 1.0, where the vehicle trail reaches the summit of a grade, there is a good area for slickrock biking gymnastics beside the trail to the south. Bikers who choose to travel this trail can follow the navigational guidance noted below for four-wheelers.

The Dragon, of the Dragonview Trail.

FOUR-WHEELING:

For four-wheeling or biking this trail, turn east from U.S. 191 about 2.8 miles south of Wilson Arch. After going through the highway fence, turn back north along the fence for about 0.2 miles, then swing right across the buried gas pipeline and back south again. The trail straight ahead along the highway fence ends in a few hundred feet at a good starting point for hiking to Lopez Arch. After a few more yards, the main trail goes down a steep, rocky slope, then descends to cross a sandy wash and climb a sizable hill with a large sandstone dome at its summit. From there, the trail descends again to cross a second wash, then climbs into the higher terrain close to the southern tip of Agate Butte. At about mile 1.6, the trail angles south and descends steeply into a major arm of Hook and Ladder Gulch. At the base of the grade, just beyond where the trail leaves a slickrock slope, the trail turn to travel upwash for another 0.5 miles, ending on the edge of a low alluvium ridge.

HIKING:

This trail is the primary access route for hiking into several outstandingly lovely tributaries of Hook and Ladder Gulch, as well as along the base of the southern cliffs of Agate Point, the high cliff-walled peninsula between the Hook and Ladder and Joe Wilson canyon complexes. The first hiking opportunity is from the end of the short trail spur. From there, hike down the slope toward Lopez Arch to the drainage, then ascend the slickrock by any feasible route to the photogenic span.

A second hike begins at about 1.3 miles from the trail start, where the trail first closely approaches the cliff. From this point, explore the cliff-base and seep-caves in the big alcove in the cliff that was visible to the north of the trail just before reaching mile 1.3.

Another much longer hike begins at about mile 1.6, just before the main trail starts descending steeply toward the wash. From this point, hike along convenient sandstone ledges, climbing up to any interesting cliff-base seep-caves and other features. This route continues around the upper end of the deepest white Navajo Sandstone drainage to the immense sandstone fin that separates two drainages of Hook and Ladder. From there, it descends the long white sandstone ridge that projects southwest from the fin to the wash bottom, then down the wash to where the obscure trail ascends back to the hike's starting point.

There are three good hiking routes from the end of the main trail. Each one explores one of the narrow, picturesque tributaries of Hook and Ladder Gulch by going up their branching drainages. It is possible to go almost to the end of the left fork, the one circumnavigated on the above hike. With a little effort, some easy chimneying and a bit of wading, it is possible to go all the way to the immense echoing alcove and plunge-pool at the end of the very narrow canyon to the east of the looming fin. The easternmost and longest tributary offers delightful hiking, with springs, pools and an obscure petrified track site, but is blocked by an enormous, impassable rockfall just beyond the springs. It is possible to hike down into a higher stretch of this long drainage from a spur of the Razorback Ridge Trail, but the luring canyon beyond the rockfall cannot be entered without rappelling down a sheer pouroff.

NOTES:

1. At one time a trail went down the wash that the last half-mile of this trail goes up, but that early trail is now so eroded and obscured by vegetation and flooding that it is virtually impossible to find and travel except on foot.

2. This trail was named for its views to the east of Dragon Rock, a huge red sandstone promontory reminiscent of a mythical dragon's head.

3. Some of the seasonal vegetation that obscures this vehicle trail as it travels in the Hook and Ladder wash-bottom is a variety of wildflowers. During the spring, such species as Globe Mallow dominate. Late summer rains bring out sunflowers and several other colorful species. In early autumn, the perennial rabbitbush adds great masses of yellow to this already brilliant scene.

Along the cliff-base hike from mile 1.6.

107

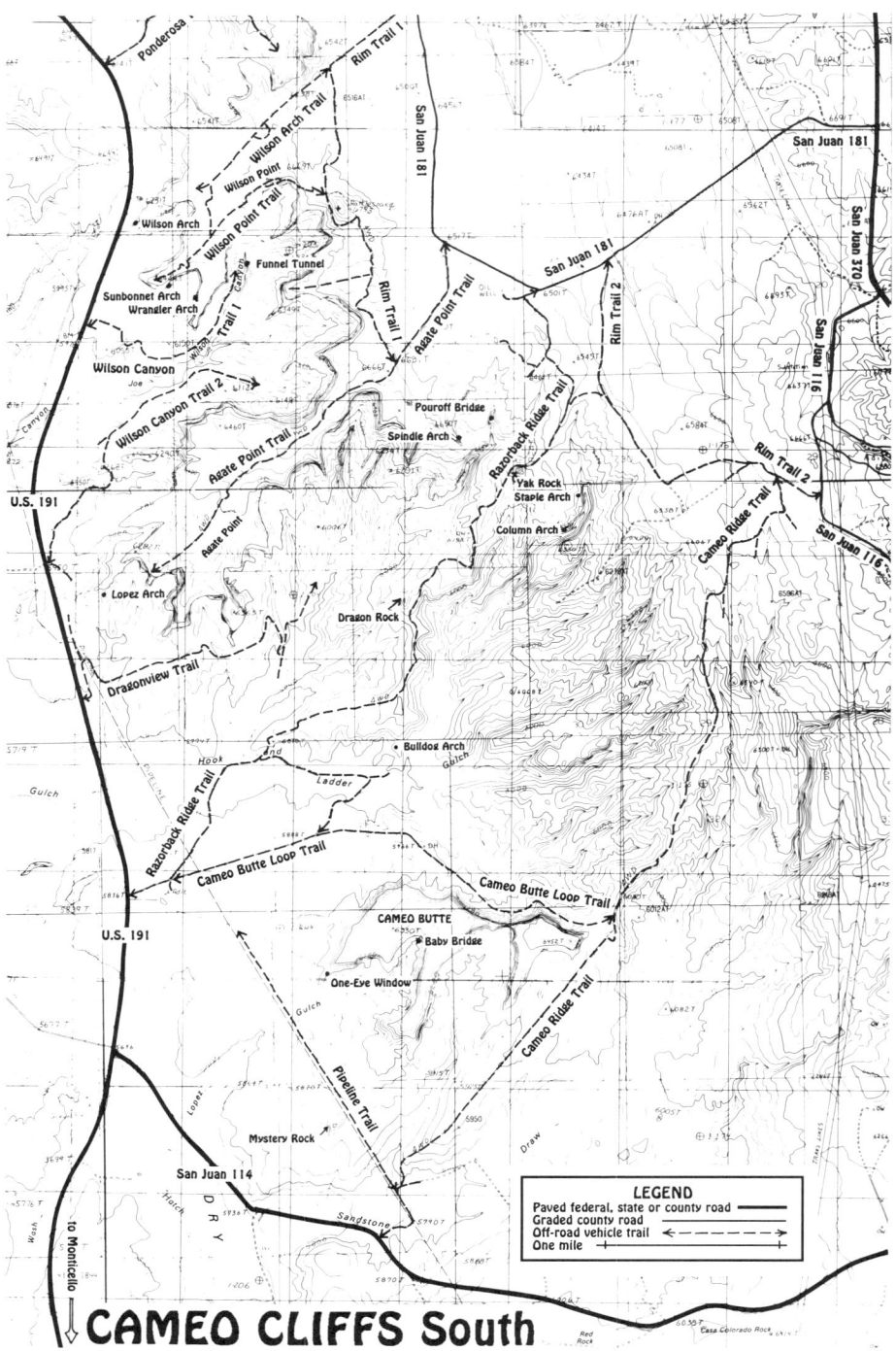

CAMEO CLIFFS South

TRAIL NAME: RAZORBACK RIDGE TRAIL

ACCESS: from U.S. 191 about 3.9 miles south of Wilson Arch, or about 1.0 miles north of that highway's junction with paved San Juan 114.

TRAIL LENGTH: about 5.3 miles to its connection with graded road San Juan 181.

TRAIL CONDITIONS: seasonally obscured wash-bottom sediments, rough slickrock, sandstone ledges, very eroded sandy deposits, and rocky packed sediments.

SUGGESTED FOR: experienced four-wheelers and bikers only.

DIFFICULTY: moderate to difficult from the U.S. 191 end, but a little easier from the San Juan 181 end, for both four-wheelers and bikers.

CONNECTIONS: connects with the Cameo Butte Loop Trail two places, and travels between U.S. 191 and graded San Juan 181.

SPURS: one short spur near the trail's northern end, plus another 1.1-mile spur that connects with the Cameo Butte Loop Trail.

View from near the Razorback Ridge Trail.

DESCRIPTIONS:

BIKING:

The rough, eroded condition of this trail make it too difficult and demanding for general biking, but attractive to bikers who enjoy challenges. The outstanding scenic views from the trail and its access to good hiking might make it worth the trouble for those who appreciate these factors, especially if traveled in the downhill direction. Either way, a vehicle shuttle would be required, unless the return trip is made via the Cameo Ridge and Cameo Butte Loop trails. Both of these trails are even more difficult. If this highly challenging loop route is being considered, it is better traveled in the counter-clockwise direction. See the description for the Cameo Ridge Trail. Bikers who wish to travel the Razorback Ridge Trail from U.S. 191 can follow the navigational guidance given four-wheelers below.

FOUR-WHEELING:

This trail is a challenging route for four-wheelers, especially when driven from its lower end, as described below. In addition to the trail conditions already noted, there are a couple of minor navigation problems. The trail is described from its lower end at U.S. 191 in the following paragraphs. See note 1 at the end of this description.

Slickrock wilderness adjacent to the Razorback Ridge Trail.

Go through the gate in the highway fence about 3.9 miles south of Wilson Arch or about 1.0 miles north of San Juan 114, and just west of a large mass of red-hued sandstone. At mile 0.2, the Cameo Butte Loop Trail goes straight ahead and a short spur goes right to a privately-owned corral and storage caves blasted out of the mass of sandstone. The Razorback Ridge Trail angles left from this four-way junction, crosses a rolling meadow, then drops down into the main drainage of Hook and Ladder Gulch. At about mile 1.2 from the highway, the trail reaches an old corral. The main trail goes closely past the corral and climbs to higher ground via a very rocky and eroded grade.

From the corral, a spur trail continues up the wash. During the warmer months this connecting spur, and its undescribed spurs, is obscured by seasonal vegetation. About 0.6 miles from the corral, this spur angles sharply right then ascends to higher ground where it connects with the Cameo Butte Loop Trail in another 0.5 miles. Bulldog Double Arch is in a short tower of red-hued sandstone on the slickrock slopes about 0.7 miles east of the old corral. Undescribed spurs of this spur trail continue toward the several upper drainages of this arm of Hook and Ladder. They are very overgrown, but could be used for closer hiking access to these canyons.

Beyond the old corral, the main trail climbs into eroded, sandy terrain then crosses an expanse of bare and very rough slickrock. The invisible trail aims toward the right side of a low ridge of sandy deposits that reaches out onto the slickrock peninsula, then climbs onto that ridge and continues on it through very eroded sandy terrain toward the big red sandstone dome of Dragon Rock. Along this stretch, the trail gradually ascends a ridge that slopes steeply down on both sides, with magnificent views in all directions.

About 0.6 miles beyond Dragon Rock, the trail reaches a small ridge of dark red sandstone, then skirts around this on a trail barely one vehicle wide, with the low ridge on one side and a drop of several hundred feet on the other. Beyond this short cliff-hanger stretch, the trail crosses a narrow place that was built up by those who originally constructed the trail, then continues toward Yak Rock, another red sandstone dome. The trail beyond Yak Rock is somewhat eroded but much easier to travel. Yak Rock was so named because from the west its profile somewhat resembles this animal.

About 0.5 miles past Yak Rock, the trail reaches a trail fork at a fenceline. The spur to the right is a rough shortcut to Rim Trail 2. The main Razorback Ridge Trail continues straight ahead from this junction to connect with a graded road just east of an oil installation, then goes right to connect with San Juan 181 in another few yards.

About 0.4 miles beyond the fenceline, a spur trail goes left. This spur ends in about 0.2 miles, but another trail spurs right, northwest, near its end. This spur ends at an old reservoir, another dry "air-pond," in about 0.3 miles.

HIKING:

This trail offers access to three suggested hiking routes and almost endless free-style hiking in the upper Hook and Ladder slickrock wilderness area. The first area worth hiking is at Dragon Rock. Explore around this immense mass of red sandstone and up onto its higher levels. There is a large and beautiful amphitheater in its northern side. This hike can be continued on the lower sandstone terraces that are still high above the northern arm of Hook and Ladder Gulch.

One access route into the upper tributaries of the southern arm of Hook and Ladder is via the overgrown trail spurs that enter their lower reaches from beyond the old corral that the main trail passes. See the trail description in the four-wheeling sec-

A cloud-shadow reveals Column Arch, center.

tion below. These canyons can also be explored from the smaller sandstone dome beyond Dragon Rock, or from the upper two miles of the Cameo Ridge Trail.

From that smaller dome there are two good hiking routes to explore. One heads east from the dome, then drops down to go around the head of another Hook and Ladder tributary, just above its spectacular pouroff, then along the canyon's far side and out onto a high sandstone point. Little Staple Arch is visible not far from this route on the western slopes above this canyon, and Column Arch is visible from the eastern side of the canyon in some tall rock columns where the canyon turns sharply. The opening in this arch is not large, but its position and configuration make it interesting. There are remnant Ponderosa pines in the eastern slopes above this canyon.

From slickrock terraces below and to the west of the smaller sandstone dome, delicate Spindle Arch is visible in the tip of the high cliff to the west. This book's cover photograph was taken from here. By ledge-hiking upcanyon around the higher rimlands of this drainage, it is possible to descend into the canyon bottom, then up the canyon toward a pouroff. This short stretch of canyon usually has at least a little water in it. Progress upcanyon ends at lovely twin slickrock pouroff alcoves. Progress downcanyon ends at another breathtaking pouroff. On down the drainage from there, but out of sight, the canyon is blocked by an enormous rockfall.

Slickrock wilderness southeast of the Razorback Ridge Trail.

It is also easy to get down into this lovely stretch of canyon from one end of the short spur that leaves the main trail about 0.5 miles from its northern end. Hike down the white sandstone drainage to the west of the spur. Little Pouroff Bridge is at the head of the pouroff that the hike described above reached from below. To get below the pouroff, terrace around to the left down into the canyon, then up or down the canyon to the described pouroffs.

Pouroff Bridge.

Still another excellent hike from this trail goes to Spindle Arch. To find the best place to start the hike, drive this trail from its San Juan 181 end. From that graded dirt road, drive a few hundred feet on toward the oil installation, then turn left, south. From this turn, park in about 0.3 miles, walk west through the sparse trees by the road to an exposure of sandstone. Hike right around this, staying on the slickrock except where forced to cross steep sandy slopes, and staying on the highest slickrock level practical. This route skirts along beautiful Entrada Slickrock slopes below a high cliffline. It eventually becomes impossible to go any farther, just below Spindle Arch. From there, go back via the same route until it is possible to get down to a lower slickrock level, then return that way. There is a delightful little seeping spring in a small alcove at this lower level, and plenty of good freelance exploring into the lower drainage. One way to return is via a small reservoir at the head of the drainage, then on back to the main trail via an eroded vehicle trail that rejoins the main trail near the hike's starting point in about 0.5 miles.

Spindle Arch.

NOTES:

1. This trail is described here starting from U.S. 191 and traveling in the uphill, most difficult direction. A somewhat shorter description of this same trail is given in the easier, downhill direction from San Juan 181.

2. The first 1.5 miles of this trail from U.S. 191 cross undeveloped private land, but since the trail is the only practical vehicle access route to a large area of public land, it should remain open to public travel. If the highway gate should be locked, or the trail otherwise closed to public travel, this should be reported to the nearest BLM office.

3. Some of the seasonal vegetation that obscures the vehicle trails that travel in the Hook and Ladder wash-bottom is a variety of wildflowers. During the spring, such species as Globe Mallow dominate. Late summer rains bring out sunflowers and several other colorful species. In early autumn, the perennial rabbit-bush adds great masses of yellow to this already brilliant scene.

4. The ridge this trail travels divides two large arms of complex Hook and Ladder Gulch, which actually has more than twenty significant tributaries. The "gulch" is divided into two major arms, each with its family of tributaries, plus several lesser tributaries to the main drainage below these arms. This extensive canyon complex is a major scenic feature in CAMEO CLIFFS South. It offers almost endless freelance hiking opportunities.

Canyon-end, below the Razorback Ridge Trail.

TRAIL NAME: CAMEO BUTTE LOOP TRAIL

ACCESS: from U.S. 191 via a short stretch of the Razorback Ridge Trail, or from the Cameo Ridge Trail about 2.5 miles from its southern end.

TRAIL LENGTH: about 3.0 miles.

TRAIL CONDITIONS: packed sediments, very rough and eroded along several stretches, rough slickrock toward its eastern end.

SUGGESTED FOR: experienced four-wheelers and bikers only.

DIFFICULTY: easy to moderate for four-wheelers, moderate to difficult for bikers.

CONNECTIONS: connects at its south end with the Razorback Ridge Trail, and with the Cameo Ridge Trail at its north end, giving this trail its name and making it useful in a challenging loop for bikers that begins and ends from the same trailhead on San Juan 114.

SPURS: In addition to spurring from the Razorback Ridge Trail near U.S. 191, there is another spur that connects with the same trail about 0.9 miles from the western end of this trail.

Bulldog Arch, near the Cameo Butte Loop Trail.

DESCRIPTIONS:

BIKING and FOUR-WHEELING:

The primary use of this trail is as a connection between the Razorback Ridge and Cameo Ridge trails, although it is highly scenic and challenging, and there is some interesting hiking from the trail as it skirts along the base of lofty Cameo Butte. Use of this trail in a loop trip through CAMEO CLIFFS South is outlined under the Cameo Ridge Trail description.

To drive or ride the Cameo Butte Loop Trail from its western end near U.S. 191, go 0.2 miles on the described Razorback Ridge Trail then continue straight ahead at the noted four-way junction. At another junction about 0.9 miles beyond the start of this trail, near the base of a large sandstone ridge, the other spur that connects with the Razorback Ridge Trail goes left, while this trail continues straight ahead. The trail gradually climbs for the next mile, crossing many eroded drainages. At one point there is a short, rough and steep detour left around a highly eroded slope. At about mile 2.7, the trail splits. Either one is suitable because they come back together on an expanse of rough slickrock. Just beyond this slickrock stretch, the trail connects with the Cameo Ridge Trail below the soaring eastern corner of Cameo Butte. To go north on the Cameo Ridge Trail, turn left at this junction. This trail is not a through trail to most four-wheel drive vehicles. See the trail's description. To go to San Juan 114, turn right at this junction. The route this way is confused and highly eroded for the first few hundred feet.

HIKING:

There are several large seep-caves in the base of Cameo Butte that can be explored from this trail, as it skirts the butte base for almost a mile. Just before the east end of the trail, a low ridge of sandstone protrudes from the cliff-base to the northeast. For a good view of Cameo Butte and the entire surrounding panorama, climb up onto this ridge and walk to its tip. There are several small but highly ornate pinyon and juniper trees stubbornly clinging to life on this barren sandstone ridge.

NOTE: The first half-mile of this trail, from its western end, crosses undeveloped private land, but since the trail is a vehicle access route into a large area of public land, the trail should remain open to public travel. If the trail is closed to public travel, this should be reported to the nearest BLM office.

HIKING DIRECTLY FROM U.S. 191

There are two types of hikes that can be taken directly from U.S. 191, without the use of special off-road vehicles. One type is where the distance along a described ORV trail is fairly short to where good hiking begins. The other type is where there is no ORV trail, but good hiking begins directly from the paved highway. Following are some suggestions.

1. **PONDEROSA TRAIL:**

   Go through the gate in the highway fence and park, then hike along the fence to the nearby cliffline. Hike as suggested under the earlier trail description.

2. **WILSON CANYON TRAIL 1:**

   Go through the gate in the highway fence and park, then hike the trail for about 0.4 miles to the first good hiking suggested under the earlier trail description.

3. **WILSON CANYON TRAIL 2:**

   Go through the gate in the highway fence and park, then hike the few yards to the trail fork and to the end of the spur trail to the right. From there, explore Lopez Pocket and the slickrock ridge above and below Lopez Arch as suggested under the earlier trail description.

Wilson Arch, from the hiking route starting at U.S. 191.

4. **DRAGONVIEW TRAIL:**

    Go through the gate in the highway fence and park, then hike the trail for about 1.3 miles to the base of the cliffs. From there, explore the cliffline and canyons below as suggested under the earlier trail description.

5. **DIRECTLY FROM U.S. 191:**

    Park at the Wilson Arch pullout. Climb up into the arch opening, then descend and explore the big cliff-alcove behind the arch. For a longer and more demanding hike, walk north from Wilson Arch along the highway right-of-way for about 0.5 miles, to where the cliff most closely approaches the highway, then find a route up to the top of the cliff. From there, hike toward Wilson Arch along the rim of Wilson Point, the large elevated peninsula formed by the cliffs to the east of Wilson Arch, toward the arm of the peninsula in which the arch formed. It is possible and safe to get close to the top of the arch, but extremely hazardous to walk on the narrow, sloping span itself.

    For views and photographs of Wilson Arch from this high rimland, continue hiking along the peninsula rim in a southerly direction, toward the tip of the peninsula just south of Wilson Arch, which offers excellent views of the span and the picturesque terrain in Canyon Rims Recreation Area to the west, including distant Looking Glass Rock, a natural opening formed by a large seep-cave in a dome of red sandstone that is almost two miles due west of Wilson Arch.

    To return to the highway, either take the same route back, or descend the steep slickrock slopes and terraces from the easternmost rim just north of Wilson Arch. This descent goes near two interesting seep-caves, and is shorter than the described ascent route.

LOPEZ ARCH

Lopez Arch is a small, round opening in a graceful fin of beautiful red-hued Entrada sandstone. The arch is visible a few hundred feet to the east of U.S. 191, about two miles south of Wilson Arch. It was named after Fermin R. Lopez, a cowboy who worked for La Sal Livestock, later Redd Ranches, for 42 years, herding cattle and sheep in the vicinity of the arch.

When Charles Redd first took over management of La Sal Livestock, he had Lopez build sturdy corrals and sheds that would last for years. Later, as an intensely loyal foreman to the Redds, Lopez was accused — then exonerated — of filing on a homestead as a "dummy" for his boss.

Lopez and his wife Adelina raised a large family, six of whom served in the armed forces. Even well into his seventies, when he could no longer ride the range, Lopez continued to busy himself around the ranch doing such odd jobs as repairing harnesses. He was active in his community and church, helping with construction of the Catholic Church building in Monticello, and was lauded for his leadership in guiding the Spanish-speaking residents of San Juan County to become valuable citizens.

The name "Lopez Arch" was officially recognized by the U. S. Board on Geographic Names in May 1975. In honor of the occasion, a dedication ceremony was held at the site of the arch, with some 150 people in attendance, including state and county officials, to pay homage to this well-liked and respected San Juan County working-man.

SAN JUAN 114 AND SPURRING ORV TRAILS

Paved San Juan 114 goes east from U.S. 191 about 8.3 miles south of La Sal Junction and Utah 46, about 5.1 miles south of Wilson Arch, or about 2.3 miles north of where paved Needles Overlook Road goes west into the Hatch Point District of Canyon Rims Recreation Area. San Juan 114 goes past the northern side of historic Casa Colorado Rock, a large mass of red sandstone about 4 miles from U.S. 191, then continues east into higher, tilted terrain that has been, and is still being, heavily developed for its mineral resources. For the recreational purposes of this book, the usefulness of this road ends about 2.0 miles from U.S. 191, where the Cameo Ridge Trail begins.

TRAIL NAME: CAMEO RIDGE TRAIL

ACCESS: from San Juan 114, about 2.0 miles east of U.S. 191.

TRAIL LENGTH: about 5.8 miles, one way.

TRAIL CONDITIONS: packed sediments, loose sand and rough slickrock, with severe erosion many places and obscuring seasonal vegetation along the southernmost 0.5 miles of the trail.

SUGGESTED FOR: experienced four-wheelers and bikers only.

DIFFICULTY: moderate for four-wheelers, moderate to difficult for bikers.

CONNECTIONS: connects at one end with San Juan 114, with Rim Trail 2 at the other, with the Pipeline Trail about 0.4 miles from its southwestern end, and with the Cameo Butte Loop Trail about 2.5 miles from the same end.

SPURS: many short undescribed mineral-search trails spur from this trail, but most have little or no recreational value.

DESCRIPTIONS:

BIKING:

The rough, eroded condition of this trail beyond the eastern end of Cameo Butte make it too difficult and demanding for general biking, but attractive to bikers who enjoy challenges. The outstanding scenic views from the trail, and its access to good hiking, might make it worth the trouble for those who appreciate these factors, especially if traveled in the downhill direction. Either way, a vehicle shuttle would be required, unless the return trip is made via the Razorback Ridge and Cameo Butte Loop trails. Both of these trails are almost as difficult. If this highly challenging loop route is being considered, it is better traveled in the counter-clockwise direction. See the following description. Bikers who wish to travel the Cameo Ridge Trail from U.S. 191 and San Juan 114 can follow the navigational guidance given four-wheelers below.

FOUR-WHEELING:

Bikers, and such low-profile backcountry vehicles as dunebuggies and four-wheel drive ATVs, can travel this trail continuously in the uphill direction for its entire length. Most four-wheel drive vehicles will find this to be impractical because of a short but very steep down-grade about 3.0 miles from the trail's southwestern end. To sample the entire trail, such vehicles will need to explore it from each end to the steep grade, then return the same way.

The steep grade that stops most motor vehicles.

The following description is given from the southwestern end of the trail, from San Juan 114. A somewhat shorter description for traveling the trail from its northeastern end appears later in this book, as a trail spurring from Rim Trail 2.

Turn east from U.S. 191 on paved San Juan 114, then turn left onto the Cameo Ridge Trail about 2.0 miles from U.S. 191. In about 0.2 miles, the trail angles left, then right at an obscure junction in another 0.2 miles. In less than another 0.1 miles, turn left at another obscure junction. The trail straight ahead here goes to a cattle development. The trail left crosses a few more yards of meadow then ascends the lower end of a narrow ridge of land that separates two major drainages. One is Sandstone Draw, the other a tributary of this large drainage that originates in the heart of Cameo Butte, the high red sandstone peninsula to the north. After ascending the lower end of the ridge, the trail crosses several patches of slickrock then continues straight along the crest of the ridge almost due northeast, toward the eastern end of Cameo Butte.

As the trail reaches the lofty and colorful butte, the trail is highly eroded where it has been cut by several cross-drainages. At about mile 2.4, the trail ahead offers two short, steep descents to a lower level. The one that swings sharply right and then down an eroded, rocky slope is the best route both down and back up. In a few more yards, the eastern end of the Cameo Butte Loop Trail goes left. The Cameo Ridge Trail continues ahead on narrow Cameo Ridge, to reach the summit of a gradual grade in about another 0.5 miles. The full-circle panoramic view from this summit is spectacular, with the several upper tributaries of Sandstone Draw to the east, Cameo Butte to the southwest, and the immense slickrock canyon labyrinth of the upper tributaries of Hook and Ladder Gulch to the north and northwest.

For those vehicles that are able safely to descend the short and very steep downslope beyond this viewpoint, the trail jogs sharply left then right at the base of the grade, then continues along the crest of narrow Cameo Ridge, angling north toward a mass of red-hued sandstone and beyond that to the left of a large white sandstone dome. The trail is very eroded and often obscure as it travels this stretch. About 1.5 miles from the base of the steep descent, the trail jogs right then left, as it is traveling through pinyon-juniper forest over packed but eroded sediments. It swings to the right, then left again in the next half-mile, then left again for about 0.2 miles to end at a junction with Rim Trail 2 in an open meadow.

To leave CAMEO CLIFFS from there, go right for about 0.3 miles, then left on the deteriorating pavement of San Juan 116, left again in another 1.4 miles on paved San Juan 370. From that junction it is 3.1 miles north to Utah 46, then 6.8 miles west to U.S. 191.

CAMEO RIDGE - RAZORBACK RIDGE LOOP ROUTE To continue from the end of the Cameo Ridge Trail and make a loop that returns to the same starting point via the Razorback Ridge Trail and the Cameo Butte Loop Trail, or to return to U.S. 191 via the Razorback Ridge Trail, go left on Rim Trail 2 from the noted end of the Cameo Ridge Trail. About 0.6 miles from the junction, Rim Trail 2 swings right. About 0.7 miles beyond this turn, an obscure connecting trail angles left across a grassy meadow, curving to the left toward a tree line. Within 0.3 miles, this rough, eroded connecting trail reaches a fenceline with a gate that is closed when there are cattle in the vicinity. The trail beyond the gate is the Razorback Ridge Trail. Go left at this junction to continue the return loop. Refer to the description of this trail from its northern end to either of this trail's connections with the Cameo Butte Loop Trail, follow the description of that trail to its junction with the Cameo Ridge Trail at the eastern end of Cameo Butte, then return to the beginning of that trail at San Juan 114. Alternately, take the Razorback Ridge Trail southwest all the way to U.S. 191.

Baby Bridge, Cameo Butte.

HIKING:

There is one good hiking route from the Cameo Ridge Trail and almost limitless free-style exploring from the trail at various points north and east of Cameo Butte. The suggested route begins about 1.5 miles from the trail beginning. Park off the trail then hike northwest toward the low wall of dark red sandstone that projects southwest from Cameo Butte. At the wall go left, following the base of the wall into the huge central amphitheater of Cameo Butte. There, ascend onto the beautifully eroded slickrock slopes of the amphitheater and continue exploring along the main wall, leaving the slickrock only briefly when forced to, then climbing back up to travel the various slickrock levels. It is possible with care to go all the way to the end of the huge amphitheater along its eastern wall, and partly around its spectacular upper end, leaving the slickrock only briefly.

From the upper end of the amphitheater, continue along the western wall, as near to its base as practical, exploring the several seep-caves there, almost to below the gigantic natural bird-head shape in the cliff near its end. From there, drop down into the white slickrock main drainage and hike down it to a tributary drainage coming in from the left, approximately between the bird-head and the end of the low red wall in the opposite side of the amphitheater. Hike up this tributary past its narrow, serpentine pouroff grotto to the red wall and on back to the hike's starting point. Allow at least five hours for full enjoyment of this hike.

The "bird-head," in the central amphitheater of Cameo Butte.

The rugged sandstone wilderness created by the northern tributaries of Sandstone Draw is accessible for free-style exploring from the vicinity of the large dome of sandstone near the trail's upper end. The immense canyon-and-slickrock wilderness formed by the eastern tributaries of Hook and Ladder Gulch is accessible from the trail beginning about 0.5 miles north of the base of the short steep grade midway in the trail.

NOTES:

1. A prehistoric "pit house," a type of dwelling, was found close to the base of Cameo Butte in 1987. It was scientifically excavated by archaeologists in 1988 and a report issued in 1989. Carbon 14 datings indicated that the site was occupied about A.D. 200. The site was about 0.2 miles from the Cameo Ridge Trail, on a sandy ridge near the base of the south-facing cliff, about 2.1 miles from the trail's southern end. Nothing remains of the site now except some gray discolorations in the nearby soils from ashes.

2. The northern end of this trail is confused by several spurring mineral-search trails. To follow the circuitous trail alignment in that area and avoid navigation problems, refer to the appropriate trail map.

"The Eyes," in the central amphitheater of Cameo Butte.

TRAIL NAME: PIPELINE TRAIL

ACCESS: from the Cameo Ridge Trail, about 0.4 miles from its southern end.

TRAIL LENGTH: about 1.6 miles, one way.

TRAIL CONDITIONS: eroded sandy sediments, a steep and rocky slope and several eroded drainages.

SUGGESTED FOR: experienced four-wheelers and bikers only.

DIFFICULTY: moderate for four-wheelers, moderate to difficult for bikers.

CONNECTIONS: dead end, connects with the Cameo Ridge Trail at its southern end.

SPURS: none.

DESCRIPTIONS:

BIKING and FOUR-WHEELING:

The primary value of this trail is to provide access to hiking around parts of Cameo Butte. To ride or drive the trail for this purpose, travel the first 0.4 miles of the Cameo Ridge Trail as described in its description. The Pipeline Trail begins at the trail junction there. From that junction, continue straight ahead on the pipeline construction trail across the wash and toward where the pipeline and trail climb steeply up a rocky slope, then straight ahead across sandy meadows, through several eroded cuts to where the trail ends at a low sandstone ridge about 1.6 miles from where it starts.

HIKING:

At mile 0.5 from the trail start, climb up onto Mystery Rock, the large mass of red-hued sandstone to the west of the trail. This is possible via either of the two slender arms of the rock that extend southwestward. Once up on the rock mass, explore its lovely contours and erosional forms, especially its southeastern wall, then take note of the three deep potholes in its northeastern end. From the highest to the lowest, their diameters and depths in feet are: 44 by 30, 22 by 11, and 62 by 24, as measured by the authors. Their approximate capacities to overflow are 341,000, 31,000 and 542,000 gallons respectively. The mystery is -- how did these enormous potholes form in the top of this isolated sandstone dome? Water standing in shallow sandstone potholes dissolves the cementing between sand granules, thus loosening them, but how were the tons of sand then removed from these deep holes?

For another view of the surrounding terrain, drive to the end of the trail and climb up onto the sandstone ridge there. To explore around the base of Cameo Butte, drive the trail to its nearest approach to the butte, then hike across the meadows to the butte's westernmost tip. From there, explore the base of the main cliffline to the northeast beyond the fenceline there, or explore the big cliff-alcove to the east. This interesting hike is explained in the following paragraphs.

Measuring the depth of the largest pothole in Mystery Rock.

From where the fenceline reaches the cliff-base, near a protruding ridge of the cliff, note the large seep-cave above the fence then continue right around the ridge at its base into another even larger seep-cave. One-Eye Window is at the top of this cave. This natural opening first formed when the two seep-caves joined. It then continued to enlarge from surface exfoliation to its present size. The opening has been measured at 4-1/2 feet high and 30 feet wide. To view and photograph the entire width of the opening, go to the right of the alcove, then climb a few yards up the sand dune there.

One-Eye Window.

From there, continue around the base of the cliff, exploring the various levels of slickrock and the many large and beautiful seep-caves in the northern stretch of the big cliff-alcove, then return to the vehicle trail and starting point via the local drainage lines. Baby Bridge is in a cliff-base drainage line in the upper end of this big cliff-alcove. Or, if time permits, continue on into the still larger south-facing cliff-alcove in Cameo Butte and explore it in the reverse direction from that described under the Cameo Ridge Trail. Allow a full day for this longer hike and the return to the starting point.

NOTES:

1. The northern cliffline of Cameo Butte can also be explored from various starting points along the Cameo Butte Loop Trail.

2. While One-Eye Window has doubtless been seen by a few stockmen, it was independently found by the authors of this book, reported to the Bureau of Land Management, photographed, measured and documented in this book in mid-1991.

One of the many large seep-caves in the smaller amphitheater of Cameo Butte.

UTAH 46 AND SPURRING ROADS

Paved Utah 46 heads east from U.S. 191 at La Sal Junction, a small development about 6.5 miles south of Hole-'n-the-Rock, or about 3.2 miles north of Wilson Arch. The highway climbs into the higher terrain to the east of U.S. 191 and thus provides easy access to the higher trails and areas of CAMEO CLIFFS. Three county roads that are useful in exploring the CAMEO CLIFFS area spur from this state highway. These are described in the following paragraphs. None of the off-road vehicle trails described in this book spur from Utah 46. To see the relationship between this highway and the other access roads in the CAMEO CLIFFS South area, refer to the map on the inside-back cover of this book.

San Juan 131

This shortcut connection between U.S. 191 and Utah 46 angles southwest from Utah 46 about 1.0 miles east of U.S. 191. It fords West Coyote Creek about midway in the shortcut. There are some small but interesting sandstone grottoes in the drainage at the ford.

San Juan 182

This graded county road leaves the highway to the right about 2.0 miles from U.S. 191. It fords West Coyote Creek within a few hundred feet, then climbs into the higher terrain to the southeast. The road through this stretch is sometimes quite eroded, but is generally passable to off-road vehicles and to carefully driven high-clearance, low-geared highway vehicles. After paralleling a rocky drainage, the road climbs steeply upward, ascending the slopes of a hill, then skirts along the base of the hill to a road junction below the tailings of a huge abandoned uranium strip-mine, about 2.5 miles from Utah 46. At the described road junction, graded San Juan 181 goes due south beyond the cattle control gate there. San Juan 182 continues on around the heavily-mined hill to make a loop, but beyond the first mile this route is so complex and confused that it is useful only to four-wheelers who enjoy the challenge of exploring a maze of trails that are highly eroded and difficult to navigate.

San Juan 370

This paved county road goes right, south, from Utah 46 about 6.8 miles east of U.S. 191. It is described in the following paragraph.

SAN JUAN 370 AND SPURRING ROADS

This paved county road is the primary access route into the higher terrain of CAMEO CLIFFS to the west of the open country through which it travels. It crosses partly developed private land but is a county road open to public travel. Two other county roads, San Juan 181 and San Juan 116, spur west from San Juan 370 at miles 2.1 and 3.1 south of Utah 46. These roads, and the off-road vehicle trails that spur from them, are described in the following pages.

SAN JUAN 181 AND SPURRING ORV TRAILS

This graded road goes west from San Juan 370 about 2.1 miles south of Utah 46. It can safely be traveled by all kinds of vehicles during dry weather, but should not be used by highway vehicles when wet from rain or melting snow. It is about 4.3 miles long between this junction and the gate at its junction with San Juan 182 at the base of the strip mine. The road goes west for about 0.5 miles then descends into lower terrain, heading generally southwest. At about mile 2.2, the road swings toward the northwest then north, to end at a gate and its junction with San Juan 182 in another 2.1 miles. Along the way, four off-road vehicle trails spur left. These are described in the following pages.

View of one arm of Hook and Ladder Gulch and the Abajo Mountains from near Rim Trail 1.

Hiking one arm of Hook and Ladder Gulch.

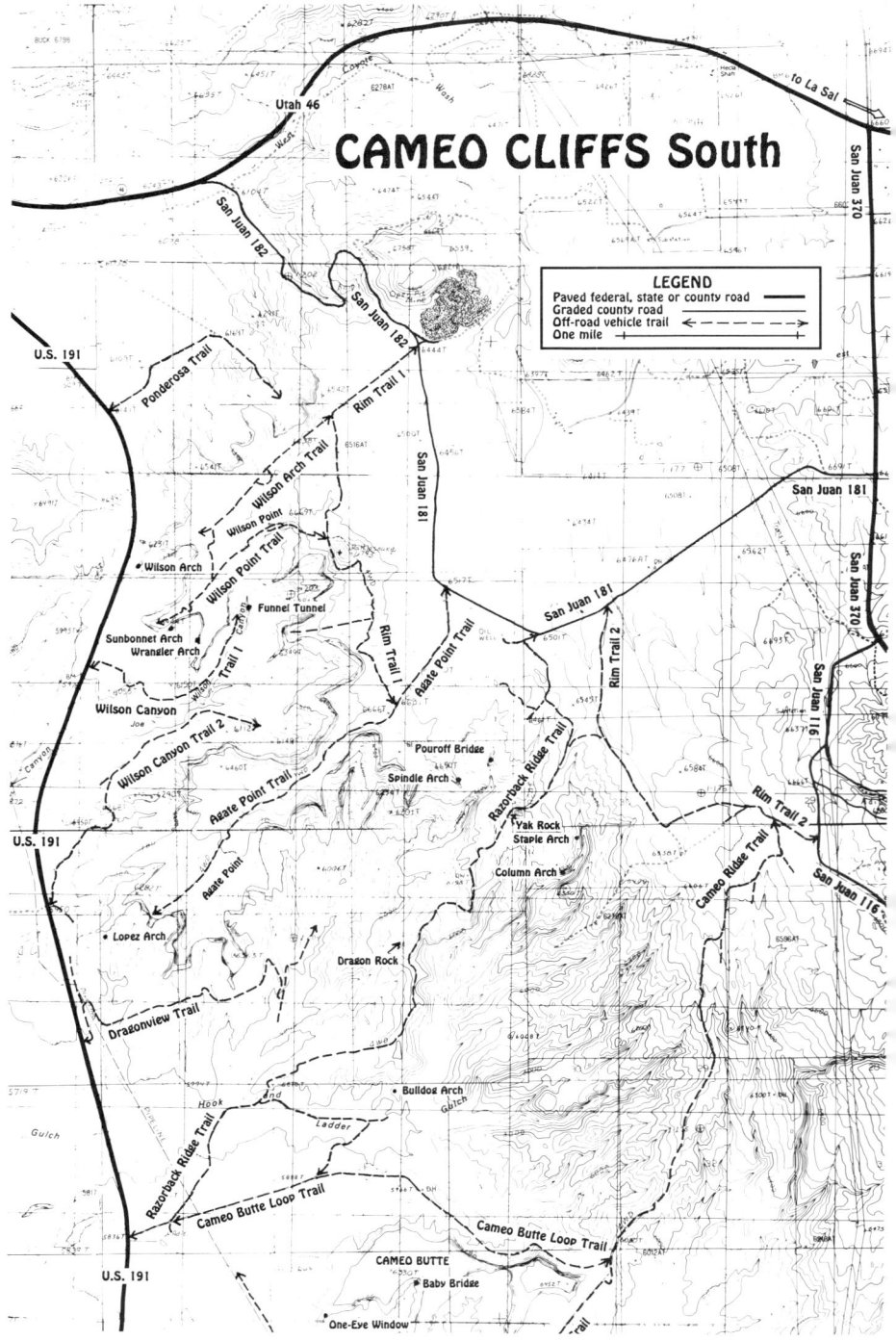

TRAIL NAME: RIM TRAIL 2

ACCESS: from San Juan 181 about 1.8 miles from San Juan 370 at the trail's northern end, and from San Juan 116 about 1.4 miles from that road's junction with San Juan 370 at the trail's southern end.

TRAIL LENGTH: about 2.5 miles, one way.

TRAIL CONDITIONS: packed sediments, somewhat eroded in places.

SUGGESTED FOR: four-wheelers and bikers and carefully-driven high-clearance highway vehicles.

DIFFICULTY: easy.

CONNECTIONS: connects with the two noted county roads at either end, plus the north end of the Cameo Ridge Trail, one short unnamed scenic spur trail and a shortcut spur to the Razorback Ridge Trail.

SPURS: two short spurs, as noted above.

DESCRIPTIONS:

BIKING and FOUR-WHEELING:

The primary use of this trail is for access to other trails. It has no other recreational use. From its northern end, the shortcut spur to the Razorback Ridge Trail turns sharply right at about mile 0.8. A short unnamed scenic spur trail goes right at about mile 1.5, where the main trail angles left. This trail ends at an overlook with good views into the complex eastern drainages of Hook and Ladder Gulch. The Cameo Ridge Trail goes right at about mile 2.2. Rim Trail 2 joins San Juan 116 in another 0.3 miles.

HIKING:

Although there are better starting points for hiking down into the Hook and Ladder canyon-wilderness, it is possible to start from the scenic overlook described above. Column Arch was first spotted from this viewpoint, but the hike to it was made as described from the Razorback Ridge Trail.

NOTES:

1. Abbreviated descriptions of the Cameo Ridge and Razorback Ridge trails are given in the following paragraphs. For full descriptions of these two trails, refer to the earlier pages describing the ORV trails that spur from San Juan 114 and U.S. 191, respectively.

2. A stretch of Rim Trail 2 plus one of its short spurs makes the connection between the northern ends of the Cameo Ridge and Razorback Ridge trails that permits traveling them as a loop.

TRAIL NAME: CAMEO RIDGE TRAIL

ACCESS: to reach the northern end of this trail, drive south from Utah 46 on San Juan 370 for about 3.1 miles, then turn right (southwest) on San Juan 116. At mile 0.8 beyond that junction, angle right, then turn right again in another 0.6 miles. This is the start of the Cameo Ridge Trail.

DESCRIPTION:

Following is an abbreviated description of this trail for purposes of navigation from its northern end. For a complete description of the trail, including suggested hiking, refer to the pages that list the ORV trails that spur from San Juan 114.

After reaching the trail start as noted above under ACCESS, the trail goes south for 0.2 miles then right (west). In another 0.2 miles, it turns right (west) again at a junction in an open meadow. In another 0.7 miles, the trail jogs briefly right then left, to continue south through pinyon-juniper forest to the right of a conspicuous sandstone promontory. Beyond that promontory, the trail descends the narrow, rocky ridge that separates the upper drainages of Sandstone Draw and Hook and Ladder Gulch. About 2.75 miles from the trail start it reaches the base of the steep grade that very few off-road vehicles will be able to climb. Beyond this grade, the trail reaches the eastern tip of Cameo Butte in about another 0.6 miles, then continues southwest in a straight line for about 1.5 miles along a ridge. It then descends into and crosses lower Sandstone Draw to end at paved San Juan 114.

TRAIL NAME: RAZORBACK RIDGE TRAIL

ACCESS: to reach the northern end of this trail, drive south from Utah 46 on San Juan 370 for about 2.1 miles, then turn right (west) on San Juan 181. At about mile 2.2 beyond that junction, continue straight ahead where San Juan 181 angles right. This is the north end of the Cameo Ridge Trail.

DESCRIPTION:

Following is an abbreviated description of this trail for purposes of navigation from its northern end. For a complete description of the trail, including suggested hiking, refer to the pages that list the ORV trails that spur from U.S. 191.

From where it leaves San Juan 181, the trail continues straight ahead for another few yards toward an oil installation, then turns left (south). From there, the trail climbs to and skirts along a ridge between the open meadows to the east and a series of drainages to the west.

Bulldog Arch, on Razorback Ridge.

About 0.3 miles from the trail start, at a point where an exposure of slickrock is visible to the west beyond a few trees, bikers will find a long stretch of bare slickrock that is good for biking gymnastics.

About 0.9 miles from the trail start, it reaches a trail junction at a gate through a fenceline. This is where the shortcut from the Cameo Ridge Trail reaches the Razorback Ridge Trail. From there, continue southwest past Yak Rock, a dome of red sandstone, on to the narrow stretch beside a low ridge of red sandstone, then to Dragon Rock, a very large dome of red-hued sandstone. Beyond Dragon Rock, the trail continues down the ridgeline, through a sandy stretch, then descends to cross a wide tongue of slickrock. Beyond the slickrock, the trail crosses another sandy stretch then angles steeply down a rocky draw to an old corral, then across broad Hook and Ladder Gulch toward another mass of sandstone. From there the trail ends at U.S. 191 in another 0.2 miles.

To reach and travel this trail as a loop from the end of the Cameo Ridge Trail, from the northern end of that trail, turn left (west) on Rim Trail 2. At about mile 1.2 from that junction, angle left across a meadow on an obscure spur trail that curves toward a tree line. In about 0.3 miles, this rough spur will meet the Razorback Ridge Trail at a fenceline. If this spur is missed, continue north on Rim Trail 2 until it ends by meeting San Juan 181. There, go left for 0.4 miles to a few yards beyond where the graded road angles right, then follow the directions in the preceding paragraph.

Hundreds of Claret Cup barrel cacti thriving on solid slickrock, Cameo Butte.

TRAIL NAME: AGATE POINT TRAIL

ACCESS: from San Juan 181, about 2.8 miles from San Juan 370.

TRAIL LENGTH: about 2.8 miles, one way.

TRAIL CONDITIONS: eroded packed sediments, sand and broken rock.

SUGGESTED FOR: four-wheelers and bikers only.

DIFFICULTY: easy for four-wheelers, moderate for bikers because of sand, especially when the trail is very dry.

CONNECTIONS: connects with Rim Trail 1 about 0.9 miles from the trail beginning, dead end beyond that junction.

SPURS: this trail has several undescribed spurs on Agate Point that are highly eroded but of some possible value for hiking access to the lofty peninsula's miles of rimlands.

View of upper Joe Wilson Canyon and the La Sal Mountains from Agate Butte.

View from the Agate Point Trail.

View from near the Agate Point Trail. Note the boulders of agate on the cliff rim.

DESCRIPTIONS:

BIKING and FOUR-WHEELING:

Agate Point is the high and isolated peninsula of sandstone between Joe Wilson Canyon and Hook and Ladder Gulch. It is defined by the sheer cliffs that loom above these drainages. To reach this trail from U.S. 191, drive east on Utah 46 for about 6.8 miles, south on paved San Juan 370 for about 2.1 miles, then west on graded San Juan 181 for about 2.8 miles. The trail begins here, at an obscure junction, by angling due south across a meadow.

About 0.9 miles from the trail start, while it is traveling through rolling pinyon-juniper forest, Rim Trail 2 goes right (north) at an obscure junction. Not far beyond this junction the trail crosses a narrows between the two major drainages that form Agate Point. There are excellent views of one arm of the Hook and Ladder Gulch drainage from near the trail along this stretch. Beyond the narrows, the trail continues southwesterly through sparse pinyon-juniper forest, passing several undescribed spurs, to end at a promontory of Agate Point high above Lopez Arch, with a breathtaking panoramic view of colorful geologic features below and in the northern districts of Canyon Rims Recreation Area to the west.

View of Lopez Arch from the end of the Agate Point Trail.

HIKING:

This trail offer excellent easy-access rim-hiking from the narrows between miles 1.2 and 1.7, and from the end of the vehicle trail. Several of the undescribed spur trails could be driven, biked or hiked toward the peninsula's rim for further rim-hiking. The views are breathtaking from anywhere along the rimlands of Agate Point.

View from Agate Butte, with Dragon Rock in the near-distance and Cameo Butte beyond.

NOTES:

1. Agate Point was named for the great masses of colorful agate that is common along its rimlands, although the same mineral also occurs throughout the CAMEO CLIFFS area.

2. The non-commercial collecting of agate specimens is permissible and a part of the recreational experience in this recreation area.

TRAIL NAME: RIM TRAIL 1

ACCESS: from the northern end of San Juan 181, at its junction with San Juan 182, and just south of the cattle-control gate at this junction, or from the eastern end of the described stretch of San Juan 182.

TRAIL LENGTH: about 2.3 miles, one way.

TRAIL CONDITIONS: eroded packed sediments and steep grades, with a 0.3-mile stretch of very rough broken rock.

SUGGESTED FOR: experienced four-wheelers and bikers only for the full length of the trail, all four-wheelers and bikers for access to the Wilson Arch and Wilson Point trails from the trail's northern end.

DIFFICULTY: easy for one mile from its northern end, from there on easy to moderate for four-wheelers and difficult for bikers, with confused navigation on its southern half.

CONNECTIONS: connects with the Wilson Arch Trail, the Wilson Point Trail, and the Agate Point Trail at its southern end.

SPURS: has one short described spur that is recommended only for experienced four-wheelers and very athletic bikers.

DESCRIPTIONS:

BIKING and FOUR-WHEELING:

This trail provides easy access to the two ORV trails that travel out onto Wilson Mesa, the elevated, multi-armed, sheer-walled peninsula that is between the Joe Wilson Canyon complex and the open meadows to the south of Utah 46. South of these two trail junctions, Rim Trail 1 offers scenic views down Joe Wilson Canyon, but is very rough, eroded and confused by other undescribed trails.

From just south of the gate where San Juan 181 and San Juan 182 meet, Rim Trail 1 angles southwest across a broad meadow for about 0.6 miles, then turns southward. At this point, the Wilson Arch Trail continues straight ahead up a steep grade. Rim Trail 1 continues south for about 0.5 miles, then climbs steeply upward for another 0.4 miles to another trail junction. There, the Wilson Point Trail goes to the right, while Rim Trail 1 angles left, to travel between the base of a rocky prominence and an arm of Joe Wilson Canyon. This 0.35-mile stretch of trail is very rocky and rough, but offers good views of the colorful canyon below.

At the southeastern end of the prominence, the trail turns right (south). From there, it reaches a junction with a spur trail that climbs steeply, then descends even more steeply out onto a scenic point between two lobes of upper Joe Wilson Canyon. Only highly experienced four-wheelers should attempt this 0.4 mile spur. From the spur junction, the main trail continues generally southward, winding along eroded slopes and through pinyon-juniper forest, to end where it joins the Agate Point Trail about 0.9 miles from San Juan 181.

HIKING:

Adventurous hikers might like to ascend to the summit of the rocky butte that the trail skirts about midway, or hike along the rimlands of upper Joe Wilson Canyon from the same vicinity. It is also better to hike the difficult described spur trail to the viewpoint at its end than to drive it.

NOTES:

1. The rocky prominence about midway along this trail is sometimes called *"Rattlesnake Butte"* from the name of the survey point on its summit. That point, at 6793 feet above sea level, is the highest elevation in CAMEO CLIFFS that can be attained for recreational purposes.

2. Traveling this trail from its southern end is not recommended because navigation from that end is very confusing.

TRAIL NAME: WILSON ARCH TRAIL

ACCESS: from Rim Trail 1, about 0.6 miles from that trail's northern end.

TRAIL LENGTH: about 1.2 miles, one way.

TRAIL CONDITIONS: very rough, steep, rocky, ledgy and eroded, with confused navigation for most of its length.

SUGGESTED FOR: experienced four-wheelers and bikers only.

DIFFICULTY: moderate to difficult for four-wheelers, difficult for bikers.

CONNECTIONS: connects with the Wilson Point Trail via a very eroded spur.

SPURS: one 0.4-mile spur that connects with the Wilson Point Trail, plus several very eroded undescribed spurs that may have some value for access to nearby peninsula rims.

From the end of the Wilson Arch Trail it is possible, but very hazardous, to hike onto the arch top.

DESCRIPTIONS:

BIKING:

This trail should be attempted only by the most athletic bikers who wish to accept the challenge of a difficult trail. For navigation, refer to the trail description below for four-wheelers.

FOUR-WHEELING:

This trail should be attempted only by experienced drivers. Long wheel base four-wheel drive vehicles may have trouble traveling the first 0.5 miles of this trail. The primary value of the trail is for wheeled access to the highly scenic northern rimlands of Wilson Point and the slickrock peninsula above Wilson Arch.

To travel this trail, go 0.6 miles on Rim Trail 1 from its northern end at the junction of San Juan 181 and San Juan 182, then continue straight ahead where Rim Trail 1 angles left (south). From this junction, the trail climbs steeply through very rough and eroded terrain, then skirts along the northern rim of Joe Wilson Point for about 0.5 miles, traveling southwest. At the rim of a small canyon, the trail swings left completely around the head of the canyon, then continues in the same alignment beyond it.

From the canyon, the trail continues through relatively level pinyon-juniper forest and is easier to travel. It ends on a rim that is still above the slickrock peninsula that Wilson Arch is in. About 0.1 miles back from the trail end, a steep, rough and eroded 0.4-mile spur goes south to connect with the Wilson Point Trail about 0.5 miles from its end. This trail is not recommended for wheeled vehicles other than mountain bikes.

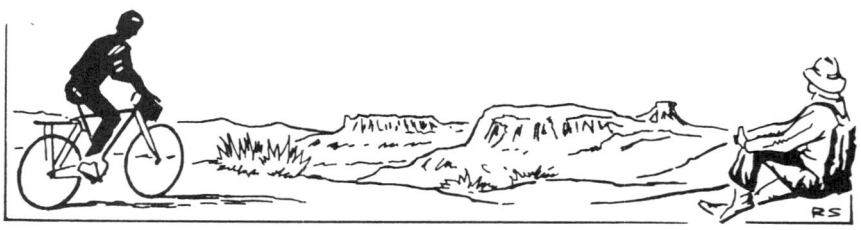

HIKING:

This trail provides several opportunities to hike short distances from the trail to the northern rim of Wilson Point. One undescribed spur trail goes for a little distance out onto a northern peninsula of the point, and a 0.5-mile hike beyond the end of the trail and down the slickrock ridge to the southwest ends at the top of Wilson Arch, but does not give a view of the span. For good views of Wilson Arch from this trail, hike south around the cliff rim onto the Wilson Point peninsula reached by the Wilson Point Trail.

NOTE: Hikers should not attempt to climb directly onto the top of Wilson Arch. The top of the span is narrow and slopes down steeply on both sides.

TRAIL NAME: WILSON POINT TRAIL

ACCESS: from Rim Trail 1, about 1.5 miles from that trail's northern end.

TRAIL LENGTH: about 1.4 miles long, one way.

TRAIL CONDITIONS: eroded packed sediments, sand, slickrock and ledges, with several short steep and rocky grades.

SUGGESTED FOR: four-wheelers and bikers only.

DIFFICULTY: easy for four-wheelers, easy to moderate with a few short difficult stretches for bikers.

CONNECTIONS: connects via a very eroded spur with the Wilson Arch Trail.

SPURS: one 0.4-mile spur that connects with the Wilson Arch Trail, plus several very eroded undescribed spurs that have little value for recreational purposes.

View of upper Joe Wilson Canyon, from the Wilson Point Trail.

DESCRIPTIONS:

BIKING and FOUR-WHEELING:

The primary value of this trail is for wheeled access to the highly scenic southern rimlands of Wilson Point and the slickrock peninsula just south of Wilson Arch.

To travel this trail, go 1.5 miles on Rim Trail 1 from its northern end at the junction of San Juan 181 and San Juan 182, then go right at the junction at the north end of Rattlesnake Butte. Within a few yards, the trail jogs left then continues in a northwesterly direction, climbs to skirt the rocky rim of Wilson Point high above the cliff-alcove formed by the main drainage of Wilson Canyon, then continues out onto Wilson Point. Along the way, the trail drops down an eroded drainage, passes the inconspicuous spur toward the north that connects with the Wilson Arch Trail, then switchbacks steeply down to a lower level and on for a short distance through soft sandy deposits and dune sand. Bikers, and some drivers, might prefer to walk the 0.25 mile from the top of the switchbacks to the end of the lofty peninsula. Beyond the trail end, the views from the peninsula rim and slickrock point to the south and west are magnificent. Wilson Arch is in clear view to the north, with the highway far below and the colorful terrain of Canyon Rims Recreation Area beyond.

HIKING:

There is good hiking along the rimland above Joe Wilson Canyon from the first mile of this trail. From anywhere at or near the end of the trail, the northern rim offers excellent views of Wilson Arch from an elevated viewpoint. From the same peninsula-tip, the colorful cliffs of Agate Point and CAMEO CLIFFS features beyond are visible to the south, while the northern reaches of Canyon Rims Recreation Area spread to the western horizon. Wrangler Arch is visible from the southern rim near the end of the trail.

NOTES:

1. The spur north that connects with the Wilson Arch Trail is about 0.5 miles back from the end of the Wilson Point Trail, but is difficult to find and travel. It is not recommended for wheeled vehicles other than mountain bikes.

2. Large quantities of native agate are exposed along the rimlands of Wilson Point. The non-commercial collecting of agate specimens is permissible and a part of the recreational experience in this recreation area.

SAN JUAN 116 AND SPURRING ORV TRAILS

San Juan 116 heads southwest then south from San Juan 370 about 3.1 miles south of Utah 46. The only use of this road is for access to the southern end of Rim Trail 2 and the northern ends of the Cameo Ridge and Razorback Ridge trails. These trails and their access from San Juan 116 were described in earlier pages and are not repeated here.

Looking Glass Rock, from the end of the Wilson Point Trail.

Wilson Arch, from Wilson Point.

153

DEDICATION

This book is dedicated to

DAVE MINOR

BLM Recreation Planner

He knew there was something special
about the Cameo Cliffs area and
wanted it to be a part of
Canyon Rims Recreation Area
but this was the best we could do
under the circumstances

Rest now in peace, Dave

INDEX OF SIDEBARS

ALBERT CHRISTENSEN, SANDSTONE SCULPTOR 18
PREHISTORIC AND HISTORIC REMNANTS 20
HISTORY OF LA SAL, UTAH 22
CAMEO CLIFFS HIKING 44
CAMEO CLIFFS WILDLIFE 47
CAMEO CLIFFS GEOLOGY 49
CAMEO CLIFFS PLANTLIFE 50
CAMEO CLIFFS ROCKHOUNDING 92
THE ARCHES AND BRIDGES OF CAMEO CLIFFS 96
LOPEZ ARCH 122

INDEX OF ROADS, ORV TRAILS AND HIKING

CAMEO CLIFFS NORTH

PERIMETER AND INTERIOR ROADS	53
U.S. 191 AND SPURRING ORV TRAILS	53
CAVE TRAIL	54
MULESHOE CANYON TRAIL	59
OLD ROAD TRAIL	65
HIKING DIRECTLY FROM U.S. 191	67
BLACK RIDGE ROAD AND SPURRING ORV TRAILS	69
BLACK RIDGE POINT TRAIL	69
HIGHLINE ROAD AND SPURRING ORV TRAILS	71
CONNECTING TRAIL	73
BROWNS HOLE ROAD AND SPURRING ORV TRAILS	75
CAMP TRAIL	77
MULESHOE POINT TRAIL	79
CONFLUENCE TRAIL	81
OLD MINES TRAIL	83
BENCHLAND TRAIL	85

CAMEO CLIFFS SOUTH

PERIMETER AND INTERIOR ROADS	89
U.S. 191 AND SPURRING ORV TRAILS	89
PONDEROSA TRAIL	91
WILSON CANYON TRAIL 1	93
WILSON CANYON TRAIL 2	98
DRAGONVIEW TRAIL	103
RAZORBACK RIDGE TRAIL	109
CAMEO BUTTE LOOP TRAIL	117
HIKING DIRECTLY FROM U.S. 191	120
SAN JUAN 114 AND SPURRING ORV TRAILS	123
CAMEO RIDGE TRAIL	123
PIPELINE TRAIL	129
UTAH 46 AND SPURRING ROADS	133
SAN JUAN 131	133
SAN JUAN 182	133
SAN JUAN 370	133
SAN JUAN 370 AND SPURRING ORV ROADS	134
SAN JUAN 181 AND SPURRING ORV TRAILS	134
RIM TRAIL 2	137
CAMEO RIDGE TRAIL	138
RAZORBACK RIDGE TRAIL	139
AGATE POINT TRAIL	141
RIM TRAIL 1	145
WILSON ARCH TRAIL	147
WILSON POINT TRAIL	150
SAN JUAN 116 AND SPURRING ORV TRAILS	152

FURTHER READING

Those who wish to know more about the unique and fascinating canyon country of southeastern Utah will find other books and maps in the *Canyon Country* series both useful and informative. They are stocked by many visitor centers and retail outlets in the region.

The listed books are profusely illustrated with photographs, charts, graphs, maps and original artwork. The maps are also illustrated with representative photographs.

GENERAL INFORMATION

Canyon Country HIGHWAY TOURING by F. A. Barnes. A guide to the highways and roads in the region that can safely be traveled by highway vehicles, plus descriptions of all the national and state parks and monuments and other special areas in the region.

Canyon Country EXPLORING by F. A. Barnes. A brief history of early explorations, plus details concerning the administration of this vast area of public land and exploring the region today by land, air and water.

Canyon Country CAMPING by F. A. Barnes. A complete guide to all kinds of camping in the region, including highway pull-offs, developed public and commercial campgrounds, and backcountry camping from vehicles and backpacks.

Canyon Country GEOLOGY by F. A. Barnes. A summary of the unique geologic history of the region for the general reader, with a list of its unusual land-forms and a section on rock collecting.

Canyon Country PREHISTORIC INDIANS by Barnes & Pendleton. A detailed description of the region's two major prehistoric Indian cultures, with sections telling where to view their ruins, rock art and artifacts.

Canyon Country PREHISTORIC ROCK ART by F. A. Barnes. A comprehensive study of the mysterious prehistoric rock art found throughout the region, with a section listing places where it can be viewed.

Canyon Country ARCHES & BRIDGES by F. A. Barnes. A complete description of the unique natural arches, bridges and windows found throughout the region, with hundreds depicted.

UTAH CANYON COUNTRY by F. A. Barnes. An overview of the entire region's natural and human history, parks and monuments, and recreational opportunities, illustrated in full color.

CANYONLANDS NATIONAL PARK - *Early History & First Descriptions* by F. A. Barnes. A summary of the early history of this uniquely spectacular national park, including quotes from the journals of the first explorers to see and describe it.

Canyon Country's CANYON RIMS RECREATION AREA by F. A. and M. M. Barnes. A description of the natural and human history and outstanding scenic beauty in the area to the south and east of Canyonlands National Park, plus a summary of its outstanding recreational opportunities.

BACKCOUNTRY GUIDE BOOKS AND MAPS

Canyon Country **HIKING & Natural History** by F. A. Barnes. A summary of the unusual natural history of the region, plus descriptions of most of the established hiking trails and a sampler of trail-less routes.

Canyon Country **OFF-ROAD VEHICLE TRAILS - Arches & La Sals Areas** by F. A. Barnes. Descriptions of most of the backcountry roads and off-road vehicle trails in these two canyon country areas.

Canyon Country **OFF-ROAD VEHICLE TRAILS - Canyon Rims & Needles Areas** by F. A. Barnes. Descriptions of most of the backcountry roads and off-road vehicle trails in these canyon country areas.

Canyon Country **OFF-ROAD VEHICLE TRAILS - Island Area** by F. A. Barnes. Descriptions of most of the backcountry roads and off-road vehicle trails in this canyon country area.

Canyon Country **OFF-ROAD VEHICLE TRAILS - Maze Area** by Jack Bickers. Descriptions of most of the backcountry roads and off-road vehicle trails in this canyon country area.

Canyon Country **OFF-ROAD VEHICLE TRAILS - Canyon Rims Recreation Area** by F. A. Barnes. Descriptions of the backcountry roads and selected off-road vehicle trails in Canyon Rims Recreation Area.

Canyon Country **OFF-ROAD VEHICLE TRAIL MAP - Arches & La Sals Areas** by F. A. Barnes. Special topographic maps showing the named roads and off-road vehicle trails in these two areas.

Canyon Country **OFF-ROAD VEHICLE TRAIL MAP - Canyon Rims & Needles Areas** by F. A. Barnes. Special topographic map showing the named roads and off-road vehicle trails in these two areas.

Canyon Country **OFF-ROAD VEHICLE TRAIL MAP - Island Area** by F. A. Barnes. Special topographic map showing the named roads and off-road vehicle trails in this area.

Canyon Country **OFF-ROAD VEHICLE TRAIL MAP - Maze Area** by F. A. Barnes. Special topographic map showing the named roads and off-road vehicle trails in this area.

Canyon Country **OFF-ROAD VEHICLE TRAIL MAP - Canyon Rims Recreation Area** by F. A. Barnes. A special topographic map depicting the roads, ORV trails and other features of the magnificent Canyon Rims Recreation Area.

Canyon Country **MOUNTAIN BIKING** by F. A. Barnes & Tom Kuehne. Background information useful to mountain bikers, detailed descriptions of 23 good trails for biking, and basic information about the other major trails in the canyon country region.

UTAH-COLORADO MOUNTAIN BIKE TRAIL SYSTEM - Route I - Moab to Loma - *Kokopelli's Trail* by Peggy Utesch. A complete mile-by-mile guide to this 138-mile mountain bike trail, with elevation charts and additional useful information.

Canyon Country **SLICKROCK HIKING & BIKING** by F. A. Barnes. Introduces an approach to hiking and mountain biking that is unique to the canyon country of southeastern Utah, then describes and gives detailed directions for reaching many places where these new forms of recreational activity can be sampled.

HIKING THE HISTORIC ROUTE of the 1859 MACOMB EXPEDITION by F. A. Barnes. A detailed guide to hiking the route of the first American expedition to enter southeastern Utah and describe the spectacular land now within Canyonlands National Park.